Argument Mining

Argument Mining

Linguistic Foundations

Mathilde Janier
Patrick Saint-Dizier

WILEY

First published 2019 in Great Britain and the United States by ISTE Ltd and John Wiley & Sons, Inc.

ISTE Ltd
27-37 St George's Road
London SW19 4EU
UK

www.iste.co.uk

John Wiley & Sons, Inc.
111 River Street
Hoboken, NJ 07030
USA

www.wiley.com

Library of Congress Control Number: 2019943909

British Library Cataloguing-in-Publication Data
A CIP record for this book is available from the British Library
ISBN 978-1-78630-303-5

Contents

Chapter 6. Annotation Frameworks and Principles of Argument Analysis

Preface

This book is an introduction to the theoretical and linguistic concepts of argumentation and their application to argumentation mining. It partly emerged from a course given at the ESSLLI summer school held in Toulouse in July 2017. Argumentation mining is now an important research and development activity. It can be viewed as a highly complex form of information retrieval. Argument mining addresses compelling application needs like those posed by complex information seeking like reasoning for or against a controversial statement, e-debate or getting to know the different aspects of a complex issue.

Argument mining has its roots in information retrieval and question answering, with a higher theoretical and practical complexity. In particular, arguments are complex natural language constructs, with several relational aspects and implicit elements, such as the premise–conclusion–warrant triad. Therefore, it is not surprising that argument mining requires high-level natural language processing technology. Argument mining requires either complex machine learning algorithms or lexical and grammatical systems, which can deal with the complexity of arguments considered in isolation and in a context with other arguments. The goal of this book is to introduce the reader to the main linguistic and language processing concepts.

Understanding how argumentation is realized conceptually and in language usually implies manually annotating argumentation components in various types of corpora. Annotations may then be used to develop linguistic data or to train learning algorithms. Annotation is in itself a challenge, because it addresses complex phenomena, which require much training to be accurately analyzed. The complexity of annotation tasks frequently entails relatively high disagreement levels among annotators and therefore the need to develop precise guidelines and methods to reach consensus.

Argument mining requires an accurate taking into account of a number of complex models and techniques from the theory of argumentation, linguistics, corpus analysis, natural language processing technology, machine learning, knowledge representation and reasoning. The software engineering aspects may also be complex, for example, to organize the different steps of a real-world system and to update it, including the management of language resources and the production of an adequate synthesis of the arguments and other textual elements that have been collected.

This book is conceived as an introductory book that can be used as a text book for undergraduate and graduate courses in linguistics, artificial intelligence or natural language processing. It may also be useful for practitioners aiming to undertake an argument mining project. It requires some basic background in linguistics, language and computer science. Most if not all the concepts of argumentation that are crucial for argument mining are carefully introduced and illustrated in a simple manner in this book. Programming samples are given in simple and readable logic programming forms. These samples can then be transposed to a large variety of other programming paradigms. Finally, a set of well-chosen references allow the reader to go beyond in different directions, either technical or conceptual. This book is therefore conceived to be accessible to a large audience of students and practitioners.

In this book, we show that linguistic analysis and natural language processing methods can efficiently and accurately be used to mine arguments. This book aims at presenting well-founded and concrete approaches, genre and domain-independent or delimited to a given domain, which can be deployed in applications. Evaluation methods provide means to measure the overall quality of a system or a resource used to train a system. This book also describes different approaches to annotate arguments in argumentative texts and debates either written or transcribed from oral exchanges. It discusses strengths and weaknesses of such approaches and provides criteria to choose an approach given application goals. Corpus annotation is frequently viewed as the basis that shapes a running system. This tasks is presented in detail in this book, after the presentation of the main conceptual and linguistic concepts of argumentation.

This book is organized into two parts. The first part, from Chapters 1–4, deals with the main conceptual notions of argumentation and argument structure in linguistics, cognitive science, logic and artificial intelligence. These areas are crucial for argument mining. Chapter 5 establishes a transition with the more technical details in Chapters 6–8, which constitute the second part of this book. These latter chapters discuss crucial aspects of the practice of bringing argumentation concepts into argument mining systems. Chapter 6 offers a detailed analysis of annotation practice, guideline elaboration and the use of annotation platforms. Chapter 7 presents a number ongoing systems. Since argument mining is still in an early developments stage, these systems are more proofs of concepts than real-world system. These systems, nevertheless, show the main challenges and possible solutions. Chapter 8 is an illustration of the concepts presented in the previous chapters. It shows, by means of some simple lexical and grammar descriptions, how to start an argument mining system. To conclude, Chapter 9 shows that argumentation is a complex process where the textual aspects presented in the previous chapters must be paired with a number of non-verbal elements such as sounds or images to allow for a real understanding of an argumentation process.

Each chapter is conceived to have a certain independence and the reader may skip those that are of less interest to him. For example, the reader can concentrate on the annotation chapter or on implementation issues, leaving aside the more theoretical considerations of the first chapters.

The reader must be aware that argument mining is still in a very early development stage. Developing a full-fledged system is still a mid- or a long-term research, which requires a lot of efforts from different disciplines. The elements presented here are those that have been stabilized and evaluated. This book contains a few elements that show the challenges still to be resolved to develop real argument mining systems and to make the results of such a mining process accessible to users.

We feel this book contributes to clarify and possibly to open new investigation and analysis directions in information retrieval in general, at the intersection of language, cognition and artificial intelligence. Argument mining covers many useful applications for our everyday life as well as more intellectual aspects of natural argumentation.

To conclude this preface, we would like to thank the French CNRS (Centre National de la Recherche Scientifique) for providing us with the adequate means and environment for fulfilling this work. We also thank very much Dr. Marie Garnier for an in-depth proofreading of the first part of this book and her questions, which helped improve the quality of the text. We would also like to thank to a number of close colleagues with whom we had joint projects or fruitful discussions. We thank, in particular, Drs. Katarzyna Budzynska, Chris Reed and Manfred Stede.

Mathilde JANIER
Patrick SAINT-DIZIER
July 2019

1

Introduction and Challenges

Argumentation is a language activity that occurs in an interactive context. It is based on an underlying set of schemes of thoughts, processes and strategies. This chapter introduces the notions of argument and argumentation, and the basic organization of an argumentative discourse. These notions will then be developed in more depth in the chapters that follow. This introduction to argumentation is oriented toward argument mining, which is the main topic of this book, therefore it is not a standard introduction to argumentation. References will allow readers to deepen their knowledge of the theoretical aspects of argumentation.

1.1. What is argumentation?

According to Aristotle, argumentation is the ability to consider, for a given question, the elements that are useful to persuade someone. Argumentation was, at that period, closely connected to rhetoric, which is defined as the art to persuade an audience. The ancient Greek argumentation and rhetoric were mainly designed for political decision making. This is why they are essentially oriented toward debates and judiciary purposes. After a long period during which rhetoric and argumentation were disregarded because they were considered as the art of trickery, in 1958 C. Perelman and L. Obrechts Tyteca [PER 58] contributed to a renewal of rhetoric and argumentation. These disciplines got a more scientific analysis. They were viewed as the development of discursive techniques that aimed at increasing an audience's support for a given thesis. The approach was that the orator who is addressing an audience needs to take into account its values, opinions and beliefs.

In more technical terms, argumentation is a process that consists in producing articulated statements that justify a given claim. A claim C results in two standpoints: C and not(C). C can therefore be associated with justifications (supports) or contradictions (supports for not(C)). An argument is composed of at least two structures: a claim and a proposition that is a justification of the claim. Propositions (or statements) that justify the claim are called supports, while those which are against the claim or tend to disapprove it are called attacks. Supports as well as attacks can be more or less strong and direct with respect to the claim. A specific facet or part of the claim can also be attacked or supported, instead of the claim as a whole.

An important point to be highlighted when it comes to argumentation theory is the ambiguity of the word *argument* in English. D.J. O'Keefe [OKE 77] distinguishes between argument$_1$, which refers to the reasons given for or against a point of view, and argument$_2$ that has to be understood as equivalent to dispute[1]. There are also confusions between attacks or supports of a claim, sometimes called arguments. In what follows, an argument is a claim associated with a justification (or support) or an attack. Finally, the term argument also refers to the elements a verb or any predicate combines with such as a subject or an object. This sense of argument is not used in this book.

Claims can be almost any kind of proposition (or statement). They include forms such as thesis, judgments, opinions, evaluations, rhetorical questions, etc., whose goal is to put forward a debatable topic. Claims can be introduced by epistemic expressions such as *I think, it seems*, or performative verbs such as *I pretend, I recommend* and their nominalizations, which indicate that it is a personal position. A claim can be stated with a strong conviction or in a much weaker way as a possibility or a suggestion. Various operators express different levels of certainty, such as *I am certain, I feel, it seems that*. Such types of expressions are typical linguistic cues of a claim. Other forms of claims include evaluative expressions, as illustrated in example (1-1).

An argument is a complex structure composed of a claim and a set of propositions that (1) support or attack that claim or (2) support or attack other propositions in that structure, which are then considered as secondary claims. In this latter case, the aim is to reinforce the strength of the propositions related to the claim or to cancel out their effect, for example, via the attack of a proposition that supports or attacks the main claim. Supports and attacks define the polarity (i.e. for or against) of a proposition with respect to a claim. They suggest a bipolar analysis of arguments since only attacks or supports are considered.

For example, given the claim:

(1-1) *Vaccination against Ebola is necessary,*

---

1 Throughout this work, the term "argument" is used as equivalent to "argument$_1$", while "argumentation" refers to the process of arguing.

statements such as:

> (1-1a) *Ebola is a dangerous disease,*
> *there are high contamination risks,*

are analyzed as supports, while:

> (1-1b) *the vaccine adjuvant is toxic,*
> *there is a limited number of cases and deaths compared to other diseases,*

are attacks.

These statements can be produced by either a single author or by several. Their strength is partly dependent on the context and on personal evaluations. Finally, the statement:

> (1-1c) *The initial vaccine adjuvant has been replaced by a much more neutral one that has no effect on humans,*

is an attack of (1-1b); it cancels out the attack to the claim produced by the initial statement.

Beside the support and attack relations presented above, propositions may also attack the inference that connects two arguments:

> (1-1d) *Ebola is dangerous with high contamination risks, therefore vaccination is necessary,*

is attacked by:

> (1-1e) *Recent epidemiological investigations show that vaccination does not stop disease dissemination.*

Supports and attacks are crucial components of argumentation, which is based on the recognition of a difference of opinion between parties: these parties express doubts about the other party's standpoint. A preliminary step is to identify differences of opinion and then the basis on which they can be resolved. Doubts may bear on a unique or on multiple ones, for example when the claim is complex or has multiple facets. In the above example (1-1b), *the adjuvant is toxic* attacks a facet of the vaccine, i.e. how it is diluted before injection. Other facets include specifically its costs and the way it has been tested on populations. Analyzing the structure of arguments and then evaluating them is the ultimate goal of argumentation. Argumentation is a complex discourse activity that must not be confused with a demonstration. Argumentation aims at convincing someone of a certain point of view, or at resolving conflicts. Argumentation relies on more shallow structures that in formal demonstration such as argument schemes, associated with norms, rules and constraints for which models are being defined.

An argumentation can be realized in a number of manners. For example, it can be a monologue, where propositions for and against a claim are developed, for example in a news editorial. In that case, the author attempts to present an overall picture of the different positions for or against that claim. He may also wish to anticipate attacks by readers. An argumentation can also occur in a dialog between two or more persons that express different points of view concerning a claim or a standpoint. This is, for example, the case of TV or online debates, deliberation and litigation situations.

Argumentation can therefore be oral or based on written elements produced using various types of media. Argumentation is mainly aimed at (1) convincing someone or a group of people of a certain point of view or (2) coming to a reasonable agreement between two or more parties about a disagreement (e.g. in mediation and deliberations).

When one argues for a given standpoint, he is the proponent of that standpoint. The actors that disagree and argue against it are called the opponents. Arguing is not demonstrating: a proponent presents good reasons to support a claim, he does not logically demonstrate that the claim is true. He simply gives good reasons that justify the claim. A demonstration, on the contrary, is based on facts, inference rules and axioms described in a formal language, whereas argumentation expresses facts and causal schemes in natural language. It follows the well-known statement uttered by a judge: *I need proofs, not arguments!*

It must be noted at this stage that argumentation is often contrasted with explanation. When one explains something to a listener, the aim is to bring new knowledge to that listener or to help him to modify his beliefs. This knowledge is hypothesized to be true and non-controversial, unless otherwise stated. An argumentation does not *a priori* bring any new knowledge to the listener: it is aimed at persuading him of the validity of a certain claim. However, in an argumentative discussion, it is frequent to have a combination of arguments and explanation. The difference between these two notions in a discourse is not easy to make: it depends on the knowledge and beliefs of the speaker and the listener.

According to several authors, an opinion is also a slightly different notion: it is a statement that is not supported by a justification. Arguments are necessarily supported by one or more justifications even if some of them are implicit. Such implicit justifications are called enthymemes.

1.2. Argumentation and argument mining

Argument mining is an emerging research area that introduces new challenges both in natural language processing (NLP) and in artificial intelligence (AI). Argument mining is a very challenging area that involves complex language resources and parsing processes as well as reasoning and pragmatic aspects. It is an analysis process that consists in automatically identifying claims and relevant propositions that support or attack these claims in dialogues or in texts found on various types of media. Then, argument mining must identify the structure and orientation of these propositions and the relations between claims and propositions. Identifying all of these features is necessary to reach an accurate automatic argument and argumentation analysis and to produce argumentation diagrams and synthesis. This is obviously a huge task that needs to be realized step by step.

Arguments, claims and associated propositions that act as justifications may take various forms in texts and debates. Because of the pragmatic nature of arguments, linguistic cues associated with these claims and their associated justifications are very diverse, ambiguous and may even be implicit. These structures may not be adjacent in a text and therefore require complex identification processes.

So far, most experiments and projects focus on NLP techniques based on corpus annotation in order to characterize their linguistic structure. The analysis of the NLP techniques relevant for argument mining from annotated structures is presented in Chapters 6, 7 and 8. AI aspects and related domain and general purpose knowledge representation aspects have not yet been given a lot of consideration because of their complexity and diversity. They will certainly be the subject of more research in the future.

Argument mining has a large number of application areas, among which:

– opinion analysis: beyond satisfaction levels, the objective is to identify why users or citizens are happy or unhappy;

– debate analysis, in oral or written form, and the detection of argumentation strategies;

– business intelligence via the detection of weak signals with arguments;

– decision making, paired with a decision theory;

– evolution of population value system analysis on the long term;

– analysis of specific strategies of argumentation: juridical defenses, pleads, mediation, deliberations, scientific or mathematical argumentation;

– detection of incoherence among sets of arguments and justifications, e.g. in juridical and technical documents.

Statements related to a given claim are difficult to identify, in particular when they are not adjacent to the claim, not even in the same text, because their linguistic, conceptual and referential links to that issue are rarely direct and explicit. As the reader may note it, argument mining is much more complex in general than information retrieval since an argument is a proposition.

Let us illustrate the difficulty to establish an argumentative relation between two utterances by means of an example:

Fact 1: *The situation of women has improved in India,*

Fact 2: *Early in the morning, we now see long lines of happy young girls with school bags walking along the roads.*

These two statements could be considered as pure facts, however, Fact 1 has the form of an evaluative expression, with the term "improved", which may potentially lead to discussions and controversies. With some knowledge of the considerations that are underlain in Fact 1, it turns out that Fact 1 can be analyzed as a claim: Fact 2 is a proposition that supports Fact 1 and therefore Fact 1 is interpreted as a claim. The reader can then note that knowledge and inferences are required to make explicit, and possibly explain, the relationships between women's conditions and young girls carrying school bags.

Let us now consider:

Fact 3: *School buses must be provided so that schoolchildren can reach the school faster and more safely.*

Fact 3 is a statement that attacks Fact 2, indeed: *these young girls may not be happy having to walk to school in the early morning,* but it is not an attack of the claim Fact 1: the facet that is concerned in the relation between Facts 3 and 2 does not concern women's conditions in particular, but schoolchildren in general.

Additional statements that are supports or attacks for the claim Fact 1 found in various texts are, for example:

Supports:

(1-2a) *increased percentage of literacy among women,*
women are allowed to enter into new professional fields,
at the upper primary level, the enrollment increased from 0.5 million girls to 22.7 million girls.

Attacks:

(1-2b) *there are still practices of female infanticide,*
poor health conditions and lack of education are still persisting,
home is women's real domain,
they are suffering the violence afflicted on them by their own family members,
women's malnutrition is still endemic.

Most of these statements illustrate how difficult it can be to mine arguments related to a claim and to interpret them. Indeed, some domain knowledge is necessary.

It is interesting to see the diversity of propositions for or against a claim, as well as their origin and how participants in a debate evaluate them and find counterpropositions or restrictions to strong propositions put forward by other participants. Here are some examples of propositions found on various forums in relation with the claim:

(1-3a) *The development of nuclear plants is a positive decision.*

Supports:

(1-3b) *nuclear plants allow energy independence,*
they create high technology jobs,
nuclear risks are overestimated,
wastes are well managed and controlled by AIEA,
nuclear plants preserve the other natural resources.

Attacks:

(1-3c) *there are alternative solutions to produce electricity with less*
pollution: coal, sea tides, wind, etc.,
alternatives create more jobs than nuclear,
there are risks of military uses that are more dangerous than claimed,
nuclear plants have high maintenance costs.

Concessions (weak supports):

(1-3d) *nuclear plants use dangerous products, but we know how to*
manage them,
it is difficult to manage nuclear plants, but we have competent persons.

In this latter set of propositions, the registers of job creation, high technology development and natural resource preservation are advocated in addition to the more standard propositions on pollution, national independence and maintenance costs. Comparisons with other sources of energy are also made, but in a relatively shallow way, which limits the strength and the impact of such propositions.

1.3. The origins of argumentation

Let us now give a few historical milestones. Argumentation has its origins in the Greek tradition, and probably also, in a different manner, in the Indian tradition. In Greece, argumentation seems to have been developed in parallel and in close connection with other major disciplines of this period, in particular geometry. Its origins are attributed to Tisias and Corax, and also probably to Aristotle (384–322 BC) and to sophists (5th Century BC). These latter philosophers had a very well-developed system of argumentation that allowed them to elaborate various types of critiques of the society in which they lived.

The Greek argumentation tradition had a lot of trends and schools. Of interest to our purpose is the Antiphonia, which was a game in which participants had to produce a counterdiscourse to a given discourse. This was an excellent exercise for students: any argument had to be transformed into a counterargument. The Greek tradition developed the notion of possible and probable and associated forms of paradoxes. From these notions, which constituted an abstraction of standard human behavior, emerged more contemporary notions such as prototypes, types and various forms of logics based on uncertainty. Finally, the tradition around Plato and Aristotle developed schemes of dialectic interactions and a critique of natural language as a means to establish forms of scientific truth. According to their analysis, natural language does not allow the demonstration of a scientific truth because it is not precise enough. Natural language is more appropriate for argumentation than demonstration.

The Greek tradition focused on rhetoric, viewed as the art of arguing. Rhetoric is based on typical language called figures of speech as well as on gestures, mimics and other features. Forms of rhetoric are detailed in Chapter 3. Briefly, an argumentation had to be structured according to the following global scheme:

– introduction;

– narration of facts, from a certain standpoint;

– argumentation (defense), with its codes and processes;

– refutation by opponents;

– conclusion, summary of the main points.

Rhetoric is composed of a form of logical reasoning (logos, the logical aspects of arguing) paired with two more subjective sets of attitudes: the ethos and the pathos, which aimed at touching the audience and producing positive affects in them in order to create a climate of confidence so that the claims could be easily accepted.

1.4. The argumentative discourse

A discourse is argumentative because of its internal organization. In argumentation, the term discourse covers different perspectives, among which (1) a local perspective, how an argument as a whole or one of its justifications, is embedded into a set of discourse structures, and (2) a global perspective, the organization of an argumentative discourse, for example to support a claim.

At a local level, an argument or its justifications are frequently associated with various sorts of restrictions that specify its scope. It may also be associated with elaborations and illustrations that make it easier to understand, and contribute to increasing its strength. Discourse structures involved at this level are those introduced by Rhetorical Structure Theory (RST) [MAN 88], which include discourse structures such as concessions, contrasts, elaborations, circumstances and conditions. The website – http://www.sfu.ca/rst/01intro/definitions.html – is particularly informative and gives a large diversity of relations with definitions and examples, for example, if we consider again the claim given in example (1-1), we may have a complex statement of the form:

(1-4a) *Even if the vaccine seems 100% efficient and without any side effects on the tested population, it is necessary to wait for more conclusive data before making large vaccination campaigns. The national authority of Guinea has approved the continuation of the tests on targeted populations.*

In this statement, the segment:

(1-4b) *it is necessary to wait for more conclusive data before making large vaccination campaigns,*

is the kernel, which attacks the claim (1-1) on vaccination, and the text portions before and after this text portion are discourse structures that insert the argument into a context and make it more explicit. This text portion can be tagged as follows:

<argument>
<concession> Even if the vaccine seems 100% efficient and without any side effects on the tested population, </concession>
<main arg> it is necessary to wait for more conclusive data before making large vaccination campaigns, </main arg>
<elaboration> the national authority of Guinea has approved the continuation of the tests on targeted populations</elaboration>
</argument>.

Restrictions on the scope of a justification may not be adjacent to the justification kernel but may appear, for example, at the beginning of a section or even in a title. These must be taken into account in the analysis of an argumentation since the restrictions they convey may change the way statements attack or support each other.

At a more global level, a discourse is analyzed as set of language acts that follow a precise organization called a plan. A discourse always has a goal that is reflected in the plan that is followed. Plans may be different for each of the main types of argumentative discourses since the aims are different. Argumentative discourses include different styles such as deliberative, judiciary, epidictic, exhortative, epistolary, advertising and propaganda.

1.5. Contemporary trends

Contemporary studies on argumentation are based on foundational works, among which those by J.L. Austin [AUS 62] and J.R. Searle [SEA 69] for their model of language acts, and works by H.P. Grice [GRI 75] for discourse models and cooperative principles.

Argumentation involves a number of areas in language, philosophy and cognition. First, argumentation is a mental process associated with a linguistic activity. Most argumentative statements have an effect on the listener or reader: they affect their thought and belief systems, possibly their psychological system. Argumentation includes norms that are followed more or less strictly. These norms allow an audience to decide whether an argumentation is sound and respects a certain balance between the proponent(s) and the opponent(s). Norms include features such as efficiency, accuracy and truth in order to avoid various forms of fallacies and trickeries. These norms are developed in the following chapter. Argumentation is also concerned with cooperativity principles: its aim is to construct a consensus around a claim. Argumentation includes identifying divergences between opponents and finding an acceptable compromise, for example, in the case of a mediation. Argumentation is a powerful means to develop critical thinking. From this picture, the reader can infer that argument mining and result evaluation is a very complex process that involves most of the resources of NLP and AI.

The recent trends in argumentation can be summarized in five main theoretical research directions:

– Pragma-dialectics, F. van Eemeren *et al.* [EEM 92, EEM 01]: argumentation is viewed as a type of dialog following strong norms. Argumentation is then considered as a means, via dialog, to resolve conflicts and to reach an acceptable consensus;

– Argumentation and Conversation, J. Moeschler [MOE 85] and E. Roulet [ROU 84]: this approach is the analysis of verbal interactions in an argumentation. Argumentation is associated with pragmatics and conversation. In their perspective, argumentation consists in discourse acts that must follow norms, rules and constraints;

– Pragmatics and Linguistics of argumentation, J.C. Anscombre and O. Ducrot [ANS 83] where new forms of rhetoric are integrated into pragmatics. A revision of the notion of argument within the fields of language semantics and pragmatics is proposed. Argumentative connectors and operators are investigated in depth: these all connect language acts that allow an audience to interpret utterances as arguments for or against a claim. Argumentation is considered as a language activity rather than a discursive process;

– Argumentation as a communicational act, J. Habermas [HAB 87]: this approach develops an ethics of argumentation and communicative actions;

– Logical Pragmatics of argumentation, J.B. Grize [GRI 90] aims at modeling natural logics and cognition within the framework of argumentation and communication. In this approach, arguing consists in modifying the beliefs and the representations of an audience.

Beside these trends, a number of authors have developed more specific analyses, among which are C. Plantin [PLA 96], L. Toulmin [TOU 03], D. Walton *et al.* [WAL 08], etc. The theoretical aspects of argumentation presented in this volume largely reflect the first two directions advocated above, namely pragma-dialectics and argumentation and conversation. They are, we feel, more central to the objectives of argument mining: identifying arguments, schemes, argument organization for example in a debate. The notion of argument scheme complements these two directions, since an important challenge of argument mining is to identify the schemes used in supports and attacks.

2

The Structure of Argumentation

In this chapter, we develop the main notions of argumentation that are central and of practical use for argument mining. Theoretical aspects of argumentation, such as the notions of argument evaluation and typologies of refutation, are not addressed in depth since they are not used in argument mining. This chapter introduces the structure of an argument following Toulmin's model, which is the standard model that is considered in most analyses. Then, the notions of agreement and disagreement are developed, showing how divergences can be represented and possibly resolved. This chapter concludes with a presentation of argumentation graphs and argumentation schemes, which are central elements of argumentation. The expressive power of Toulmin's model based on warrants and backings is compared to the power of argument schemes with the goal to clarify the contribution of each of these foundational approaches to argumentation.

The notions presented in this chapter are of a particular interest for argument mining: for example, identifying how argument schemes are used in a given argumentation contributes to the evaluation of that argumentation.

2.1. The argument–conclusion pair

Let us first develop the basic structure of an argument. We start by going over the main terminological variations found in the literature about argumentation in order to avoid any ambiguity.

Claims, also called conclusions, are basically rational statements. They are in general the expression of a fact or of an event, a prediction, a judgment, an evaluation, a thesis, a piece of advice or a warning. The main point in argumentation is that whatever form a claim has, it is always possible to express some form of doubt about it. Two standpoints originate from a claim: the claim itself and its negation.

The negated form of the initial claim may get supports or justifications that are attacks of that initial claim.

Given two utterances E1 and E2, the relation:

Premise (E1) – Conclusion (E2)

is the kernel or the basic unit of an argument. In this configuration, we say that the premise justifies, gives reasons for or supports the conclusion. The conclusion is the claim, sometimes called a stance. In a monologue, the premise may appear first, as in the example (2-1) below, to give more strength to the conclusion, which then seems more natural:

> (2-1) *Vaccination prevents disease dissemination, therefore vaccination against Ebola is necessary.*

The construction premise–conclusion can be realized explicitly by clues such as:

E1 motivates, defends, induces to believe, implies, therefore, causes, explains, proves, E2, etc.

or, conversely:

E2 given, because... E1.

When several premises are developed to support a conclusion, it is frequent that the conclusion appears first so that the reader knows where the premises lead to. There is *a priori* no precedence constraint between an argument and a conclusion.

A premise and a conclusion or a claim and its justification are necessary components for an argument to be identified. Without a justification, a claim is often viewed as an opinion. In other cases, the justification is so obvious that there is no need to mention it, for example, *do not spray flowers with a negative temperature.* Finally, note that the terms premise–conclusion must be used with care because they suggest a logical relation that does not exist in argumentation. A justification simply attempts to give reasons that support a claim.

2.2. The elementary argumentative schema

This section presents the standard model of an elementary argumentative schema. It then discusses the nature and the different organizations of arguments in an argumentation.

2.2.1. *Toulmin's argumentative model*

In this section, we present the standard argumentative schema proposed by S. Toulmin [TOU 03]. Let us again consider the basic argumentative element:

P $\Rightarrow$ C. (Premise/Conclusion)

which can be illustrated by:

(2-2) *It's freezing this morning $\Rightarrow$ flowers will suffer.*

This construction is supported by a passage or justification rule W, called the Warrant, for example:

W = *frost deteriorates flowers.*

The warrant justifies why the premise entails the conclusion. This simple construction is usually represented by the schema given in Figure 2.1.

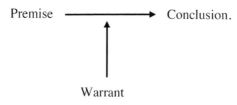

Premise ⟶ Conclusion.

Warrant

Figure 2.1. *Basic Toulmin's model*

Two additional notions are usually added to this initial scheme: (1) "Backing", which is a general rule that explains the warrant, and (2) "Rebuttal", which allows exceptions to the claim. This latter notion is crucial in argumentation since an argumentation is not a demonstration and therefore can suffer exceptions.

The example above can then be extended as follows:

(2-3) Fact or premise: *It's freezing this morning,*

Conclusion: *flowers will suffer,*
Warrant: *plants in general do not like frost,*
Backing: *physical law in botany,*
Rebuttal: *unless they got early sun or were well protected.*

This more elaborated construction is usually represented by the schema given in Figure 2.2.

The main notions used in this schema can be summarized as follows with the various synonymous terms found in the literature:

– claim or conclusion: the statement that the speaker wants the listener or reader to accept, as much as possible;

– premises, justifications, reasons, grounds, facts, stance or evidence: the data and facts offered to support the claim;

– warrant: connects the grounds or justifications to the claim, it mainly justifies the support relation or "inference" from the grounds to the claim. Warrants are in general accepted as truths that apply to a large range of circumstances;

– backing: supports and explains the warrant, it provides trustworthiness to the warrant. A backing is therefore a general rule, such as a physical law;

– qualifiers: these are statements about the strength of the claim. Qualifiers specify the confidence an arguer has in his/her claims. Qualifiers are often provided to the claim via the grounds through the warrant. They may also apply to grounds or evidence. They may also question the validity of Rebuttals and counterarguments;

– rebuttals: these are exceptions to the claim. Rebuttals develop situations in which a claim may be defeated. Rebuttals are sometimes called or viewed as counterarguments.

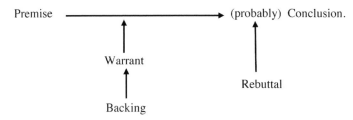

Figure 2.2. *Comprehensive Toulmin's model*

Some remarks can be made on how these notions are used in a concrete manner in real argumentations. First, qualifiers are often implicit since authors do not state the probability of their claim in the data. Sometimes adverbs of certainty are used such as *probably, certainly, most probably*. Then, the warrant is generally implicit: the logical explanation why one should accept the claim is not given, at least in a comprehensive manner. It is part of general knowledge shared by most if not all participants to a debate. Therefore, mining for warrants has not been developed so far. The rebuttal can be generalized to various forms of refutations and attacks. Backing provides evidence to support the claim, but it does not explain the reasoning that is used and the knowledge associated. It is stated by the author as a fact.

Toulmin's model and the associated terminology are frequently felt to be too close to a logical reasoning schema, which typically leads to a conclusion inferred from a number of elements and justifications. The propositions in a logical deduction are assumed to be true or false. In an argumentation, this not necessarily the case: propositions are not assertions. They do not have a truth value *a priori*. Justifications are not the same as the premises of logical systems: they are more shallow and are subject to debate. Therefore, arguments as well as opinions are basically speech acts of a pragmatic nature.

2.2.2. *Some elaborations and refinements of Toulmin's model*

In some frameworks, different categories of claims are identified. The aim is to show that different forms of strength may be identified depending on the type of claim. Another aim is to make the use of specific argumentation schemes more straightforward (see section 2.5).

A claim is a point an arguer is making, a proposition he or she wants someone else to accept. Three types of claims, with different functions, have been identified:

– fact-based claims that focus on empirical phenomena that can be verified via observation, experimentation, statistics or any other data-supported analysis;

– judgment or value claims that involve opinions or subjective evaluations of various kinds;

– policy-based claims based on actions that should be taken in a given circumstance.

In several approaches and also when mining arguments, various forms of evidence are formulated. They provide a kind of rationale for the claim or the stance being made. They include statistics, reports, physical evidence, etc. When it exists, evidence must be explicitly stated in texts or debates.

A warrant connects one or more justifications to a related claim. In such a schema, it is possible to have several warrants involved, each of them developing a particular link between each justification to that claim. In general, they must form a coherent set of statements. Similarly, a warrant may be backed by one or more backings.

In the abundant literature on argumentation, several types of warrants have been identified. The goal is to have a better understanding of the role of warrants and to deepen the relationship between evidence, or justifications, and claim. The most commonly admitted categories for warrants are the following:

– Generalization warrant: extends what is true for a sample to what is likely true for a larger population;

– Sign warrant: characterizes evidence as a sign, a symptom or a clue;

– Authority warrant: characterizes authoritative sources in support of the claim: this is close to some argument schemes based on authority or expertise;

– Analogy warrant: develops analogies of similar situations or events to support the claim;

– Causality warrant: characterizes the evidence or the justification as being caused by the claim,

– Principle warrant: characterizes the use of a broader principle that is relevant to the situation at stake.

Some of these categories may be conjoined or may interact in the connection between a justification and a claim.

2.2.3. *The geometry of arguments*

An argumentation is a structured set of arguments and propositions developed around a claim. Secondary claims may appear in an argumentation, with their own justifications. Arguments use objects or facts and relations between them. Argumentation is based on the structure of reality, as perceived by listeners and speakers. For example, the most frequent relations are based on analogy or causality.

Arguments and argumentation undergo language constraints and their possible pragmatic effects. This includes the presence of prerequisites, side effects, distortions, ambiguities and forms of implicitness. Argumentation is basically an interactive process, where human factors, either positive or negative, play an important role. Such factors include, for example, ease of expression, expertise, reliability and authority. Finally, argumentation is not a logical deduction, it is therefore not based on formal deduction rules. Argumentation uses various types of argumentation schemes whose aim is to model the argumentation activity in a less formal way than logical deduction would.

Communication rules in any type of argumentative interaction require to make explicit every element in a discussion. However, as in any natural language communication, deliberately keeping some premises or conclusions implicit cannot be avoided. Deliberately leaving implicit premises or conclusions may be part of an argumentation strategy. Antagonists may indeed infer different unexpressed or implicit elements that they would accept with less hesitations. From:

The vaccine is toxic,

antagonists may infer their own reasons that they think are true and will therefore not question or refute other statements such as:

(2-4) *because the adjuvant is toxic,*
because the vaccine is unstable after some time, etc.

Communication rules state principles, among which are *be clear, be sincere, be efficient, keep to the point.* The goal is to make the argumentation process as clear, objective and balanced between parties as possible. However, given the nature of language and the importance of presuppositions, which cannot be avoided, communication rules still allow the existence of unexpressed elements but suggest that they be made as accessible as possible to the other party. These rules should apply to any type of speech act.

A claim or a standpoint may be supported or attacked by means of one or more statements. In that case, it is recommended to make all premises explicit. Arguments may be organized in different manners, among which the following constructions are frequently observed:

– *Multiple premises*: This construction consists in using several alternatives to defend or attack a claim; these multiple premises do not depend on each other and their weight may be different. For example:

> (2-5) Conclusion: *You cannot get vaccinated against Ebola in Monrovia.*
> Premises: *The vaccine against Ebola is not available;*
> *Monrovia is not accessible to visitors.*

These two premises have a high weight, determining which one is the strongest is a matter of personal evaluation.

– *Coordinative premises*: These consist in the conjunction of statements that form a homogeneous whole. These statements depend on each other in several ways, their structure is *a priori* flat as in most coordination structures. For example:

> (2-6) Conclusion: *We had to go to a restaurant for dinner.*
> Premises: *The fridge was empty and all stores were closed.*

These two premises are connected by a causal relation: food must be bought (consequence of: the fridge is empty), but it cannot since stores are closed.

– *Subordinative premises*: These consist in chains of statements, where a statement justifies the previous one. This can be viewed as sequences of arguments. These statements are structured as layers. Some statements in the chain may become subclaims related to subargumentation. The weakest statement determines the strength of the whole. Subclaims can be supported or attacked. For example:

> (2-7) Conclusion: *I cannot help you to repaint your house.*
> Premises: *I have no time: I have to prepare exams: otherwise I will lose my financial support, etc.*

In terms of acceptability and strength, it is probable that, *a priori*, more statements entail a higher acceptability level. These three different constructions can be mixed, leading to a relatively complex argumentation graph.

Within the framework of argument mining, one of the challenges is to detect the type of argument structure from language realizations. Language clues are not necessarily explicit, in that case, knowledge (domain, common sense) may greatly help. Identifying the type of argument structure that is used is crucial in order to evaluate the global orientation of the argumentation.

In a well-constructed argumentation, connectors and other clues contribute to the identification of the argumentation structure. Some typical clues are as follows:

– multiple premises: *apart from, not to mention, another reason, aside from,* etc.;

– coordinative premises: *as well as, in addition, on top of that, especially, not only, more importantly,* etc.;

– subordinative premises: *because, therefore, since, that is why,* etc.;

– closing clues: *to conclude, to summarize, I conclude that, taking everything into consideration, all things being considered,* etc.

2.3. Modeling agreement and disagreement

Statements may attack or support a given claim. In this section, different models and typologies of supports (which are forms of agreements) and attacks (disagreements) are presented. Identifying agreements and disagreements in argumentation is a major task in argument mining. We also introduce rules and strategies to resolve disagreements since their identification is an important matter in argument mining.

2.3.1. *Agreeing versus disagreeing*

Given a claim, statements either support or attack it by means of various forms of agreement or disagreement expressions. This view is called the bipolar analysis of statements: a statement either attacks or support a claim. It may also be neutral or irrelevant. This view remains the main trend in argumentation, although there are a few other types of analysis.

An argument is the expression of a doubt (attack) or of approval (support) with respect to a statement, a part or a facet of a statement, a statement presupposition, or with respect to another argument, for example:

(2-8) *vaccination prevents bioterrorism,*

supports issue:

Vaccination against Ebola is necessary,

on the facet that a disease with high contamination risks can be used as a weapon. In terms of argumentative strength, a statement that is supported by another one gets a higher strength.

While agreement is often marked by a causal relation or an analogy between the claim and the statement, disagreement frequently uses various forms of negation, or negatively oriented terms, or develops contradictions with the claim. Contrastive connectors such as *but, however* may be used to express disagreements.

In a debate, an agreement between two parties can be developed on a proposition possibly supported by other participants to the debate. Similarly, a new disagreement on any proposition or argument may arise at any point during a debate and results in the use of new doubt expressions. In the evaluation of arguments as well as in argument mining, it is crucial to be able to separate the main differences of opinion from the subordinate ones. For example, here are three arguments attacking claims, and which themselves subsequently undergo an attack. These attacks are not necessarily adjacent to the argument in a debate or a text:

(2-9) *Ebola: The vaccine is too expensive for poor countries ... when large volumes are produced, it will be much cheaper and accessible to everyone,*

(2-10) *Nuclear power: There are risks of military uses ... the AIEA controls wastes and production,*

(2-11) *Gender equality: Practices of female infanticide still persist ... but stronger and independent control has been implemented in each village via nurses.*

In (2-9), the claim on the necessity of the vaccine against Ebola is attacked by the first proposition, on the topic of its cost, then a second proposition attacks that first proposition by stating that the cost issue will be resolved via massive vaccine production. The second proposition is still hypothetical (future tense); it is therefore weaker than the first one, which is not canceled out.

In terms of evaluation, either the second proposition that attacks the first cancels out the first proposition's impact on the claim, or it weakens it if the second one is judged not to be as strong as the first one. In more logical terms, we say that the first argument is defeated by the second one, which remains, so far, undefeated. Longer chains of attacks or supports can be observed that have an impact on the defeated status of each argument.

To conclude, in an argumentation, statements may attack each other, in that case, if they have the same strength, they cancel out their impact on the claim. If they have a different strength, the stronger one wins and is kept as a support to the claim, since it attacks an attack. Obviously, the notion of strength remains to be clarified, as we discussed it further in Chapter 3. For example, let us consider the following elements again:

(2-12) Premises: *Nuclear: there are risks of military uses,*

(2-13) Attack 1: *no, because the AIEA controls wastes and production,*
Attack 2 of Attack 1: *but the AIEA is largely controlled by the military.*

If Attack 2 is judged to be stronger than Attack 1, then Attack 1 is canceled out and Attack 2 becomes a support of the claim since attacks of attacks become supports. An argumentation is represented by an argumentation graph (e.g. Figure 2.3) where all the relations between statements are made explicit. It is then possible, for each statement, to define its defeat status by taking into account its environment, in particular whether it is supported or attacked by others and with what strength.

The main levels of disagreement between statements or between a statement and the main claim can be roughly defined as follows, starting with the strongest form *a priori*:

– refutation of the main point of a statement or a claim, as illustrated above;

– identification of an error in the statement; in this case, an explanation is provided that clarifies why the statement is incorrect, e.g. *nuclear plants use fewer natural resources than other electricity production plants* can be attacked by *nuclear plants use a lot of water to cool down reactors, and this water may become polluted* that clarifies why the initial statement is incorrect;

– elaboration of a contradiction with supporting evidence from facts, e.g. *nuclear energy is safe* attacked by evidence from facts: *14 nuclear plants in France have rusty pipes*;

– elaboration of a contradiction but with no or little evidence; this is akin of a "language game" that shows that the opposite also makes sense, e.g. *vaccination is necessary* versus *no, vaccination is unnecessary in most countries*. This contradiction develops the two standpoints related to the initial claim;

– criticism on the way the statement is uttered (its form, the terms used), without considering its content, e.g. the form of *nuclear energy is a good thing* is criticized by *what you mean by "good thing" sounds fuzzy to me;*

– attack of the person who is making the statement (*ad hominem*): incompetence, lack of reliability, untruthfulness, etc., e.g. *this scientist published fake results in the past to please companies, why should I believe him?*.

Although this hierarchy introduces different levels of disagreement, it is possible, for example, for an *ad hominem* attack to be as strong as the refutation of the main point of a statement, for instance when it can be shown that a statement is made by someone who is well known to be dishonest. Finally, from the point of view of language, the distinction between each of these six levels can be clearly identified from linguistic clues. The difficulties are in the identification of statements and in the analysis of the nature of the refutation as will be developed in Chapters 3, 6 and 7.

2.3.2. *The art of resolving divergences*

Argumentation may occur in very diverse situations, from a personal internal debate on a decision to make to mediation and open public debates. In this latter case, the proponents and opponents may be quite numerous and with various interests, beliefs and strategies. Whatever the number of participants to a debate, some stability in argumentation strategies is observed.

Debating and possibly resolving divergences is one of the main aims of argumentation. For that purpose, a number of rules, norms and constraints have been elaborated with the goal to support valid and optimized debates. The starting point of this elaboration are the cooperative principles, most notably developed by P. Grice [GRI 75] in his four maxims. Cooperative principles describe how and how efficiently communication can be achieved in everyday situations, via any kind of medium, and more specifically how listeners and speakers must act cooperatively and mutually try to understand the other party's views.

The first of Grice's maxims is the Maxim of Quality that requires speakers not to say anything they believe to be false or for which there is a clear lack of adequate evidence. The second maxim is the Maxim of Quantity that requires speakers to be as informative as possible but not more than is required. The Maxim of Relation requires speakers to be relevant and therefore to avoid digressions and comments that are not in the discussion topic. The goal is to keep to the point in a relevant manner. However, relevance is a notion that is difficult to characterize in concrete situations. It may depend, for example, on the assumptions and beliefs of the listeners. Finally, the Maxim of Manner requires speakers to avoid obscure expressions, ambiguities and various forms of prolixity. These maxims aim at describing the assumptions listeners make about the way speakers will argue in cooperative situations, which is not necessarily the case when the speaker wants to influence the listener.

In argumentation, at the language level, the constraints are to only use formulations that are clear and as unambiguous as possible in order to avoid confusions and misinterpretations. In particular, implicit elements, indefinite references, unfamiliar terms and vague or underspecified concepts or constructions must be avoided. The use of future tenses, negation, complex noun phrases (NPs) or highly embedded clauses is not recommended because of the risks of ambiguities these constructions may induce in the listener's mind.

Grice's maxims are at the origin of a large part of the norms and rules developed by several authors in argumentation, among which is van Eemeren's group [EEM 92, EEM 01]. Having an in-depth knowledge of these norms and rules is important to understand the structure of an argumentation, in particular when it contains fallacies or various types of trickeries. They are also important to evaluate the overall quality of an argumentation by identifying its conclusions. These norms and rules are summarized in the following paragraphs.

First of all, three principles indicate how claims and related statements should be expressed:

1) an attack or a support must always be clearly related to a claim that has been uttered: one should not shift topics, one should not use fake doxa (facts that are supposed to be known and accepted as true by everybody), and one should not misrepresent or simulate a fictitious claim uttered by the other party;

2) defend only your own claim: develop relevant propositions (justifications), do not abuse of authority, otherwise the risk is to develop an irrelevant argumentation, which may rather play on pathos (pathetic fallacy);

3) one should not falsify or deny an unexpressed premise that is not really ambiguous or vague. Implicit elements are frequent in communication, there are many implicit premises, but they must be well known to everyone or easy to infer.

Next, in the course of a debate, several rules must be applied to preserve a well-balanced debate that would lead to conclusions deemed acceptable by all parties involved. These can be summarized as follows [EEM 01]:

1) do not prevent the other party(ies) from giving claims and standpoints and from expressing doubts. In particular, do not pressure or throw discredit on other parties, do not attack their credibility, integrity and personal interest;

2) when a standpoint is uttered, it must be defended by its utterer if that person is asked to do so. Speakers must not shift the burden of proof. Speakers in a debate must organize sequences of standpoints if there are several and must not forget any. It is recommended in this situation to start with the most straightforward standpoints, where arguments will have the heaviest weight. This does not mean, however, that they will be easier to defend;

3) do not violate a starting point: do not present a premise that is not the accepted starting point, or do not deny an accepted starting point;

4) apply an appropriate argument scheme otherwise a standpoint may not be conclusively defended, do not use inappropriate schemes (use populist fallacy, confuse facts with judgments, make hasty generalizations, develop false analogies, use incorrect cause–effect relations, etc.);

5) the reasoning model used in the argumentation must be logically valid (e.g. do not confuse necessary and sufficient conditions).

Finally, when all arguments have been developed, a conclusion should be formulated. Principles suggest that:

1) a defense that fails results in the retraction of the corresponding claim or standpoint;

2) a defense that succeeds must result in the retraction of the antagonist's doubts;

3) however, frequently, conclusions are not so clearcut and boolean: facets may succeed for a standpoint while others succeed for the other(s). It is also possible for the defense of all standpoints to fail. In both cases, it is necessary to elaborate a kind of compromise, where, for example, the facets that can be admitted for certain standpoints are kept, provided that the conclusion is coherent.

2.4. The structure of an argumentation: argumentation graphs

An argumentation can be represented by a graph that shows the attacks or supports related to a claim and also those that hold between statements. A typical example is given in Figure 2.3, with claim CLAIM and statements A1, A2, B, D, E, F, G, H, J and K. Dashed arcs indicate attacks, whereas arcs with a continuous line indicate supports. For example, B supports the claim and is attacked by D. If D has the same strength as B, then the support effect provided by B is canceled out by D. A1 and A2 may be coordinated statements (see section 2.2.3) that form a whole supporting the claim. H supports the claim, it is supported by K, but attacked by F and J. As a result, and depending on the strength of F, J, K and H, the effect of H on the claim may be weaker or stronger. K and H are subordinated statements: they form a chain that, in our case, supports the claim.

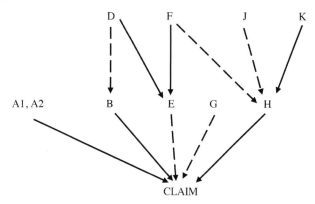

Figure 2.3. *An argumentation graph*

As explained above, the elaboration of an argumentation follows a number of norms and principles, independently of its form (text, debate, mediation, etc.), and its domain follows a number of norms and principles. These differ substantially from those used to construct demonstrations. The literature has developed a number of discussions on the validity of these norms and principles. From these discussions emerged the notions of paralogism and fallacies.

For example, a paralogism can be an argumentation that does not meet the rules of syllogisms, even if it resembles a valid syllogism:

(2-14) *The French are often on strike,*
Some professors are French,
therefore some professors are on strike.

A third term such as,

therefore some professors may be on strike,

would be more acceptable.

On the other hand, fallacies are typically based on an incorrect form of deduction, for example a situation where there is no relation between the first two statements in spite of their common language form:

(2-15) *A genius is never understood,*
no one understands me,
therefore I am a genius.

Fallacies and paralogisms occur in particular when there is:

– a misuse of a formal deduction rule or technique;

– a misuse of induction rules;

– an incorrect form of analogy, when reasoning by analogy;

– an incorrect conclusion from statistical analysis;

– the reference to false observations;

– the reference to possibly incorrect beliefs.

To overcome these problems, a number of authors developed specific approaches. C. Perelman *et al.* [PER 58, PER 77] defined quasi-logical argumentations, where argumentation is based on the structure of reality, elaborated, for example, by means of relations between objects, or via causality. The central point in Perelman's approach is that inferences structure reality, which should limit fallacies. S. Toulmin *et al.* [TOU 03] defined nine types of argument processes based in particular on analogy, generalization, cause, authority, opposites, degree, etc. These are relatively close to the notion of argument schemes. These processes guide the construction of arguments in a sound way to avoid fallacies and paralogisms. F. Van Eemeren *et al.* [EEM 92] developed 10 rules of critical discussion leading to the notion of *argumentation contract*. The objective is to reach a reasonable and well-balanced consensus between parties, avoiding incorrect arguments from being formulated.

2.5. The role of argument schemes in argumentation

2.5.1. *Argument schemes: main concepts*

From these approaches emerged an operational analysis of how argumentation develops. For that purpose, argumentation schemes have been introduced. These are patterns that describe informal inferences relating premises to a conclusion. Argumentation schemes reflect the argumentative structures used in everyday conversation where a speaker is attempting to get a listener to come to accept a conclusion. Schemes are patterns that model argumentative informal reasoning, including reasoning with uncertainty and lack of knowledge. There are different categories of argumentation schemes, based on different types of data, among which:

– schemes based on symptomatic relations where a standpoint is defended by citing a sign, a symptom or a specific mark typical of the argument: a typical feature, property, quality, etc.;

– schemes based on analogies where something in the standpoint is also cited or generalized in the statement(s): the standpoint should be accepted from this analogy. In an analogy, an element X in the standpoint and another element Y in the statement share a large number of major characteristics;

– schemes based on causality: a standpoint is defended by a causal connection with a statement, such that the standpoint should be accepted on the basis of that connection.

The most comprehensive and advanced set of schemes is presented in [WAL 08]. A number of refinements have been developed for specific classes of schemes in, for example, [PAR 08]. A first set of schemes concerns those constructed from the notions of analogy, classification and precedent. A second set includes schemes where knowledge, practical reasoning and notions such as consequences and alternatives are central. A third set includes schemes based on generally accepted opinions. The fourth and last set includes schemes based on causality, causation, effect to cause and correlation. An important feature of schemes, since they are not as strict as logical deduction, is that they are in general associated with critical questions. The role of these questions is to measure the strength of the scheme that is used in a precise situation: some questions may indeed reveal the fragility of a scheme by their scope.

Using argument schemes is a well-known argumentation process; it is an efficient approach to argue, allowing for the identification of unexpressed premises. Argument schemes also contribute to the evaluation of the strength and the scope of arguments. Given propositions which are related by these schemes, the objective is then to check for pragmatic and logical inconsistencies: each argument must be valid and it should be possible to make unexpressed elements, called *enthymemes*, explicit in the argumentation. Beside argument validity, an important task is to identify which argument schemes are used, and how they link premises to claims or standpoints. When argumentation schemes are identified, argument validity can be evaluated in context. The aim is to detect types of incorrect argumentative discourse: each element of an argument must be acceptable, logically valid and the argument scheme used must be appropriate, otherwise the argumentation is not fully valid and therefore acceptable. More generally, the soundness of an argumentation depends on how schemes are used.

Automatically identifying schemes is now one of the main challenges in argument mining. Annotating schemes to be able to automatically identify them may also entail revisions of scheme classifications, since these may have fuzzy limits. Although argument mining is still in an early development stage, several projects have been aiming at automatically identifying the argument schemes used in a debate or in written documents [GRE 17, FEN 11]. This is a crucial task for the construction of an argumentation structure and for a concrete evaluation of the outcome of debates, including how norms have been used. Schemes are difficult to identify in general because linguistic marks tend to be sparse, vague or ambiguous. Some examples are given in the second part of this book, where schemes are annotated.

Automatically evaluating the soundness of an argumentation in practical situations is extremely complex. Theoretical models have been developed, but the gap between these models and the reality of argumentation is large. This gap includes the modeling of specific forms of reasoning and knowledge representation. This is so far a relatively remote aim of argument mining, where experimentation and evaluation will have major roles to play.

2.5.2. *A few simple illustrations*

The notion of argument scheme can be illustrated with a few simple cases. More elaborated schemes are discussed in the following sections.

The argument scheme *Trust from Direct Experience* [PAR 08] can be formulated as follows:

if A and B are two protagonists, let us assume that B utters proposition P. Then, according to this scheme, if A knows B to be reliable, then A may decide that B is trustworthy concerning P. As a result, A accepts and validates P.

This scheme has fuzzy elements that can be questioned, for example:

(2-15) *How well does A know B? How much is B an expert of P? How trustworthy is B concerning P (e.g. he may defend his own interests)?*

The proposition P can be defeated if one of these questions cannot be answered appropriately. Additional questions include:

(2-16) *Is P consistent with what other sources or authors say? Is P based on evidence and, if not, how has it been elaborated?*

The scheme *Trust from Expert Opinion* is relatively similar to the previous scheme:

A knows that B is an expert of a domain D, and P is a typical proposition related to that domain. Then, assuming that B utters P, A may decide that P can be accepted.

Similarly to the previous example, this scheme raises several questions, among which:

(2-17) *How credible is B concerning D? How much typical of D is proposition P? Is P consistent with what the other experts of D may assert? How trustworthy is B concerning P?*

The following schemes are typical of arguments based on the nature of things or practices. The argument scheme *from Example* is a scheme in which a claim is supported by providing examples which are typical of that claim. Questions include:

(2-24) *Are the examples typical? How strong is the generalization?*

The argument scheme *from Popular Practice* says that if a large majority of people does A or acts as if A is the right thing to do, then most people think A, and A is probably right.

If we consider a argumentation genre that includes deliberations, the scheme *Deliberation ad Populum* is based on the following rule (which has several variants depending on the context):

A group G of people has deliberated extensively, accurately and as intelligently as possible on proposition A. They all accepted proposition A. Therefore, A is probably true. Extensions include the prestige of belonging to G for any external person P who also accepts A.

The reader may note that schemes characterize ways of arguing, and that these ways can be challenged and defeated since they are quite a remote form of logical deduction.

2.5.3. *Argument schemes based on analogy*

There are several argumentation schemes *based on analogy*. Let us review a few cases and their associated critical questions.

The argument scheme that describes a *deductive form from classification* is the simplest form of analogy. It says that if all G's are classified as F's according to our own current knowledge of entities, then if *a* is a G then *a* is also an F.

Roughly, a typical scheme based on *analogy* says that if proposition P is being debated and if proposition P′ is known to be true and if P and P′ share a lot of similarities, then P must be a valid proposition to construct an argument. This scheme is rather vague, with little explicative power. There are various ways to express analogy, and analogy can be more or less strong, as can be noted in the utterances:

P is similar to P′, P and P′ are of the same type, etc.

As an illustration, let us consider:

(2-21) P: *In an introduction, examples must be simplified,*
Opposition: *simplified examples are useless,*
Analogy with P′: *examples in medical introductory courses are recognized to be helpful,*
Refutation by analogy: *in this course, simplified examples are useful.*

The refutation of the analogy rule is based on the fact that everything may be vaguely analogous to everything. The *ad hominem* character of analogy is strong: the opponent may accept the analogy, but may go further by elaborating a point in the analogy that contradicts the conclusion. For example:

(2-22) *P: Should methadone be reimbursed by health insurance services?*
Yes, because treatments against alcohol are also reimbursed,
ad hominem refutation: *no, because methadone can lead to addiction itself.*

There are several types of analogies in argumentation: in the juridical domain, reference is made to previous or similar cases (jurisprudence); in political discourses, the notion of parangons plays a major role (major historical situations), and in moral cases we can observe a large diversity of situations, such as the following example:

(2-23) *My sister gave me my favorite comic-book as a present, it is normal for me to help her study for her math exam.*

2.5.4. *Argument schemes based on causality*

Numerous arguments refer to various forms of *causality*. A few are reviewed in this section.

The argument scheme *from Cause to Effect* says that generally if A occurs then B occurs, where A and B are events. The main questions that arise are:

(2-18) *How strong is the causal link between A and B? How similar are A and B and can we conclude on their co-occurrence?*

The argument scheme *from Established Rule* says that for all X if A is the rule for X, then (except in specific cases) X must do A. Several questions may arise on the validity and the scope of such a scheme:

(2-19) *Is it possible that there are several rules A_i instead of just one?*
If so, we may raise doubts on the most appropriate one to use.
How frequent are specific cases and do they alter the generality of the rule?

Next, the argument scheme *from Evidence to a Hypothesis* roughly says that if A (hypothesis) is true, then B (a fact, an event) will be observed to be true. Questions such as:

(2-20) *Could there be some other reason for B to be true that is not related to A?*
How strong and comprehensive is the hypothesis A?

may be raised.

Finally, this class of schemes based on causality includes schemes that are weak and must be treated as defeasible and presumptive because the links between the conclusion and the premise(s) can easily be questioned. The scheme *from Correlation to Cause* says that:

There is a clear correlation between A and B. Therefore, A causes B.

Critical questions include:

(2-21) *Is there a significant number of instances of that correlation?*
Is the relation from A to B or from B to A?
Is it possible to have a third factor that would correlate alone A and B?, etc.

More schemes are presented in the second part of this book, dedicated to annotation processes for argument mining. As the reader may note, the linguistic marks used to define, and therefore to identify the argument schemes illustrated in this chapter, are not very diverse or typical of a precise scheme, or even of a class of related schemes. It follows that automatically identifying schemes is a delicate task that requires taking into account additional resources, or that should be limiting the identification to a few, well-identified schemes.

2.6. Relations between Toulmin's model and argumentation schemes

Toulmin's model of argumentation presented above in section 2.2 and the notion of *argument schemes* presented in section 2.5 are two major but very different ways to model argumentation. Little has been said about their possible cooperation to explain the facets of an argumentation from different perspectives. However, this analysis is useful for argument mining and leads, as shall be seen below, to meaningful discussions that help understand the mechanisms of argumentation and its levels of abstraction.

This section develops a few examples to compare the expressive power of each of these two systems and shows how they converge or, conversely, contribute to explain argumentation from two different facets. Let us concentrate on the notion of warrant and backing for Toulmin's model and on a few typical and frequently used argument schemes. At this stage, it is clear that argument schemes are more generic than warrants that account for precise situations.

2.6.1. *Warrants as a popular opinion*

Let us first consider an example, which is further developed in Chapter 4 (section 4.1):

Arg1: *This hotel is very nice because it is close to bars and cinemas.*

This argument can be justified, for example, on the basis of a warrant W1. W1 is itself based on, for example, the backing B1. There are, obviously, many other possible warrants and backings, more or less generic. W1 and B1 can be formulated as follows:

W1: *It is pleasant to stay close to social and cultural activities,*

B1: *humans generally want to live in a dense social context where they have a high feeling of satisfaction and fulfillment.*

Let us consider the definition of the argument scheme *from popular opinion* given in [WAL 08, p. 311]:

1) A (any kind of statement) is generally accepted as true;

2) if A is generally accepted as true, then it gives a reason in favor of A;

3) there is a reason in favor of A.

Although this scheme is not extremely convincing to develop an argument in a real debate, it shows the differences between deduction and argumentation, which relies on relative forms of evidence.

In the above example, A is the warrant W1. This warrant is used to support the causal link given in Arg1 above:

Conclusion C = *this hotel is very nice* because W1,

where the premise *it is close to bars and cinemas* is an instance of W1 (or W1 subsumes the premise). It is important to note that the conclusion C is not expressed in the argument scheme. Then, it follows that a scheme that validates a warrant W1 can be used to establish the validity of an argument on the basis of W1. This can be expressed by a rule or principle of the form:

> C because W1 where W1 subsumes the premises of the argument Arg1.

An argumentation scheme is thus a very abstract formulation where warrants, which are more concrete, can be used as elements of the scheme, in the above example, the statement A. The argument scheme "from popular opinion" is relatively neutral with respect to the persons who have the opinion at stake. It can therefore be considered as the "by default" scheme. However, if the opinion is associated with specific classes of persons such as experts, then a scheme, probably with a higher strength, such as the argument scheme "from expert opinion" can be considered. Other schemes of interest, which are developed below include schemes "from established rule" and "from best explanation".

The same analysis can be carried out for the opposite argument of Arg1 (see section 4.1):

> Arg'1: *This hotel is horrible because it is close to bars and cinemas*,

with a warrant such as:

> W'1: *public places with bars and cinemas are very noisy and unsafe.*

If W'1 is accepted as a popular opinion, then the conclusion of the argument follows.

The ontological status of the warrant can be debated: it can be an opinion, a commonly admitted view, possibly without any real foundations, a hypothesis, the result of the analysis of an expert, a position that has been debated among various groups of people, a norm or an established rule, etc. However, some of these statements A can be in contradiction with established norms. These categories have a relatively similar behavior:

1) a statement A must be widely accepted by a diversity of means;

2) A subsumes or is largely related to a warrant or a set of warrants that support a certain argument being considered;

3) then, by virtue of A being widely accepted, W gets the same status and the conclusion C of the argument is accepted and justified by the warrant.

2.6.2. *Argument schemes based on rules, explanations or hypothesis*

These schemes share some similarities with the argument scheme "from popular opinion", however, they include additional considerations such as contextual factors of facts that are of much interest.

The version given below of the argument from established rule is given in [WAL 08]. No critical questions were formulated for this version of the scheme. This scheme is stated as follows:

1) if rule R applies to facts F in case C, conclusion A follows;

2) rule R applies to facts F in case C;

3) conclusion: in case C, conclusion A follows.

Let us consider the argument:

Arg2: *Brexit is good for the UK because citizens want a healthy economy.*

This argument may be based on several warrants, more or less generic, such as:

W2: *Citizens want to live in optimal conditions* or

W'2: *Isolating a country is the best way to get a healthy economy.*

Let us now consider the argument scheme from established rule. In this scheme:

1) R is W2 or W'2;

2) facts F are *citizens want a healthy economy*;

3) C is the context of the UK;

4) given these elements, if R = W2 or W'2 applies or is the rule, then A follows:

Brexit is good for the UK economy.

This example, although quite simple and straightforward, shows the difficulty to establish a correspondence between the rule R and a warrant W, and the identification of facts F and context C. In general, rules R are more general than warrants W; there must exist a kind of subsumption relation, where R is more generic than W. Facts are related to the central point of the argument.

Let us now consider the argument scheme from *best explanation*, which can be formulated as follows, keeping the above notations:

1) if explanation E applies to (explains) facts F in case C and is shown to be the best explanation (recognized by a majority of persons for example, or to be the most plausible), conclusion A follows;

2) explanation E applies to (explains) facts F in case C;

3) conclusion: in case C, conclusion A follows for facts F.

This scheme applies to the above example, where the rule R becomes the explanation E. It is not necessarily easy to make a distinction between rules and explanations in this context. An explanation is based, in general, on practical considerations and some form of reasoning that lead to E. A rule is more abstract and is not necessarily justified or even illustrated.

Finally, the argument scheme from *hypothesis* is similar to the two schemes above, with the reference to a hypothesis H instead of a rule R or an explanation E. A hypothesis is in general weaker than a rule and probably also weaker than an explanation, but this depends on the nature and contents of the hypothesis H. The interesting point is that a certain form of strength can be introduced in the way a warrant W supports an argument Arg, but this remains highly contextual. For example, if a hypothesis is formulated by an expert, it may have a stronger weight than if it had been formulated by a novice in a domain. The same situation holds for an explanation provided by an expert. A stronger form of support, not based on hypothesis, but on a deliberation, can be provided by the argument scheme from *deliberation ad populum* and its variants. This scheme is developed in the next section.

2.6.3. *Argument schemes based on multiple supports or attacks*

The version given below of the argument scheme from *deliberation ad populum* and its variants are borrowed from [WAL 08, p. 312]. No critical questions were formulated for this version of the scheme. This scheme is stated as follows:

1) everybody in group G accepts A;

2) group G has deliberated intelligently and extensively on whether to accept proposition A or not;

3) conclusion: therefore, A is (plausibly) true.

There are several other forms of deliberation ad populum that take into account, for example, the kind of persons in group G or the way the deliberation was conducted.

The scheme presented in this section is rather neutral from this point of view and is the most adapted to our presentation. The goal is to show that in this kind of scheme a conjunction of coherent warrants or a generalization of these warrants, if it can be defined, can be considered and discussed in the deliberation. This is of much interest since a decision is usually made by weighting different elements for or against a claim.

Before defining the role of such warrants, let us illustrate this scheme. Let us consider the following argument:

Arg3: *Vaccination against Ebola is necessary because it prevents the disease dissemination.*

In the deliberation or debate that has been carried out, the following supports and attacks may have been given; these may be partly of fully relevant with respect to the claim:

Supports:

vaccine protection is very good;
Ebola is a dangerous disease;
there are high contamination risks;
vaccine has limited side effects;
there are no medical alternatives to vaccine, etc.

Attacks:

there is a limited number of cases and deaths compared to other diseases;
seven vaccinated people died in Monrovia;
there are limited risks of contamination;
there is a large ignorance of contamination forms;
competent staff is hard to find and a P4 lab is really difficult to develop;
vaccine toxicity has been shown;
vaccine may have high side effects.

Relatively "low"-level warrants can be formulated, which, more or less, correspond to one or a few supports or attacks, for example:

W3: *It is necessary to protect a population against major diseases.*

W'3: *It is important to care about side effects of medicines.*

Then, the deliberation may consist in comparing and weighting these different warrants. It is also possible to reach a consensus on a more generic warrant that could, as much as possible, include and synthesize the different supports and attacks that have been advocated in the deliberation. For the examples above, a generic warrant such as the following could be formulated:

W″3: *It is advised/important to have a good management of medical situations to make good decisions, e.g. possible side effects, incurred costs, to protect a population.*

This more generic warrant suggests a few cases so that it is easier to understand and to adhere to. Note that the modal that is used (*advised, important*) may result from the deliberation. It is given here as an illustration.

A first conclusion of this presentation is that the statement or rule A presented in an argument scheme such as the scheme from *deliberation ad populum* is that A can be associated with several, possibly weighted, warrants. In this example again, the warrant system is analyzed as an instance of the rule R, hypothesis H or situation A advocated in the scheme. It allows to give more credibility and practical foundations to the scheme. The reader has probably noted the proximity between schemes: there is indeed, to our feeling, a kind of coherent continuum between them.

2.6.4. *Causality and warrants*

The version given below of the argument scheme *from cause to effect* and its variants are borrowed from [WAL 08, p. 328]. Several critical questions are formulated for this scheme that illustrate the difficulty to define the cause–effect pair. As for many schemes, this scheme is the generic one and has several variants. The scheme is stated as follows:

1) generally, if A occurs, then B will (might) occur;

2) in this case, A occurs (might occur);

3) conclusion: therefore, in this case, B will (might) occur.

Let us now investigate and illustrate how warrants operate in this scheme. The first difficulty is, given A and B, to ensure that they are related by a kind of causal effect, not, for example, by a mere temporal organization where two events may just temporally follow each other without any causal link *a priori*. This is not easy because the causal dimension is frequently shallow and can be debated.

To illustrate this argument scheme, let us consider the following argument:

> Arg4: *Women's living conditions in India have improved, this is due to the fact that increased percentage of literacy among women is observed: at the upper primary level, the enrollment increased from 0.5 million girls to 22.7 million girls in 5 years.*

This argument clearly establishes the link between the improvement of living conditions and the increase in literacy level. In addition, the support is reinforced by an illustration that gives statistics on school enrollment.

In this argument, B is the improvement of living conditions, and A is the increase in literacy level. The cause–effect link is clear and hardly debatable, even if other factors may interfere with this improvement. A straightforward warrant for this example could be:

> W4: *Higher education means better social and professional living conditions.*

In that case, the warrant is an instance of the cause to effect relation. The warrant is then an instantiation of the variables A and B in the scheme.

The above presentation shows some of the interactions between argument schemes and warrants and backings. The subsumption relation is relatively straightforward conceptually in most cases, however, it may be difficult to detect from a language point of view where formulations can be substantially different. The same analysis could be carried out for other classes of argument schemes, such as arguments *from alternatives* or arguments *from appeal to fear*. When warrants are explicit in arguments, it may then be of interest to annotate them: they could contribute to the induction of the type of argument scheme that has been used.

3

The Linguistics of Argumentation

There is a great diversity of argumentative texts, among which are news editorials, judicial deliberations, blog posts and radio or TV debates. Texts may originate from oral transcriptions, with limitations on the oral features (see Chapter 9). An argumentative text is generally organized around a main claim and possibly a set of secondary claims. When the text is long or complex, it may include several main claims found in different text sections, which may be related or not. This is the case, for example, in political debates where different topics may be addressed. Statements for or against these claims are developed in the text. These statements may also appear in various types of discourses that are not argumentative, for example in texts that are factual or that develop an explanation on a given topic. It is their relation with a claim that gives them their argumentative orientation.

Given a text, the problem is then to be able (1) to identify if it is argumentative and, if so, (2) to identify claims, hierarchies of claims, and their related supports and attacks. All supports or attacks do not have the same importance: they are more or less strong and central with respect to a claim. Secondary or peripheral statements with respect to a claim are probably less useful than the most central ones. The overall argumentative organization of a text is called an argumentation.

It is not easy to identify arguments and the structure of an argumentation in a text. First, most arguments are not stated as clearly as Toulmin's model suggests it. This model is in fact not frequently used in corpus analysis of arguments. Next, domain or general purpose knowledge is often necessary to identify claims and their related justifications. Finally, claims can have very diverse language forms with more or less typical linguistic cues.

In argument mining, supports or attacks of a given claim are generally searched in a variety of texts that are related to that claim. For example, concerning opinions on political decisions or product properties, attacks and supports are found in, for example, blogs, news editorials, specialized journals or consumer opinion platforms. Mining such attacks and supports spread over several sources is even more difficult than mining them in a single text where reference problems and lexical variations are less important.

From a conceptual point of view, a claim is a proposition that is credible and plausible, but not a proposition that can be shown to be true. It must always be possible to argue against a claim, i.e. to support its opposite. Next, a statement interpreted as a justification must be related to a precise claim. Justifications do not exist without any corresponding claim. Arguments, composed of a claim and of one or more justifications, are speech acts of a pragmatic nature.

Natural language has a strong expressive capability: it allows speakers to formulate an idea in a large variety of ways, including the use of metaphors, implicit references, allusions or indirect discourse. Natural language is a powerful means of developing an argumentation, but identifying arguments is a very challenging task for annotators. Then it is not surprising that annotator disagreements are high and that automatically identifying arguments is very challenging (see Chapter 6).

In this chapter, dedicated to the linguistic dimensions of argumentation, section 3.1 addresses the linguistic structure of claims, then section 3.2 deals with the linguistic structure of supports and attacks. Claims, supports and attacks share a large number of linguistic cues and constructions. Then, section 3.3 addresses the analysis of the strength of a statement based on language cues. This analysis includes the taking into account of discourse structures and of the argument scheme that has been used. This chapter ends with a presentation of the various facets of rhetoric, which are important in argumentation.

3.1. The structure of claims

Claims may have a large diversity of forms: a fact, a thesis, an opinion, a judgment, a position on a topic, a question, a rhetorical question, etc. Claims must have a debatable character: they express something that is plausible but may be questioned in various ways. This plausible character is often realized by means of evaluative terms or expressions. Statements become claims when it is possible to find related justifications or attacks. This section presents the main linguistic cues that are typical of claims. However, a number of claims are not marked by any linguistic cues: their argumentative character is pragmatic. Furthermore, some of these linguistic cues can also be found in justifications and other types of pragmatic constructions, which makes the identification of claims difficult.

The first difficult point in claim identification is to delimit the text span that could constitute a claim. In general, it is a sentence, ending with a full stop, an exclamation or a question mark. A claim may be longer if it includes restrictions, comments, definitions or circumstances of various kinds. A sentence may also be composed of several claims, possibly hierarchically organized, for example:

> *Due to the necessity of a systematic vaccination against Ebola, the authorities of country C have decided to reduce the funding of education in English.*

This statement contains two potential claims (*systematic vaccination* and *funding reduction*), which can be equally debated. Furthermore, the causal link between the two can be also debated. If the vaccination necessity is attacked, then the latter claim is also attacked. The need to delimit claims has led to the emergence of a research topic, as well as the notion of argumentative discourse unit (ADU), derived from the notion of elementary discourse unit (EDU) in discourse analysis. ADUs are segments that, in general, contain an argument, a claim, a support or an attack.

Claim delimitation is addressed in Chapter 6, which is dedicated to argument annotation. So far, it is essentially an experimental process based on annotations, even if cues such as punctuation, connectors and relative clauses can be taken into account.

The second challenge is to identify statements that have a debatable character. This identification can be realized partly by analyzing the linguistic elements in the statement, which introduce this debatable character. A first set of linguistic cues are those that are proper to the content of the claim. These cues include, but are not limited to, the following:

– Scalar adjectives such as *easy, difficult, efficient, unsafe*, which have an evaluative dimension in the context of a claim. These adjectives evaluate a property or a characteristic that is central to concepts of the claim or of closely related concepts. For example, in:

> *Vaccine development is very expensive, the adjuvant is toxic,*

expensive evaluates the property "cost" of the vaccine, which has the general properties of artifacts such as costs and functions. In the second claim, where *adjuvant* is a derived concept, which refers to a part of the vaccine that is injected, "toxic" refers to a more indirect property of medicines, for example, their "side effects". Evaluative adjectives can also appear in comparative expressions:

> *electricity produced from nuclear energy is cheaper than electricity produced from coal or wind.*
> *Nuclear wastes are more dangerous than coal wastes.*

Boolean adjectives are less frequent since they tend to express a position that is more definitive: *Ebola vaccination must be compulsory...*

– Verbs that have a clear positive or negative polarity, e.g. *to protect, to prevent, to damage*. This polarity introduces a flexible character that easily suggests discussions and debates.

– Adverbs that focus on specific features such as necessity, obligation and possibility such as *necessarily* and *inevitably* where these features can be debated. Adverbs associated with the notions of frequency or completion are also frequent in claims since the level of frequency they induce can be debated, e.g. *generally, almost never, seldom, rarely*.

– Modals and modal expressions that convey an idea of possibility or plausibility such as

> *might, should, would, could be* and *should be possible*;
> *the vaccine against Ebola should be compulsory in infected areas.*

In Romance languages, conditional and subjunctive modes are also used to convey plausibility.

– Forms such as *why should* that typically introduce rhetorical questions:

> *Why should citizens save money? To support SMEs.*

In this example, the debatable segment is the response provided by the utterer.

– Typical types of punctuations such as exclamation marks:

> *Let our committee make a decision!*

Such a statement, if not ironic, could be followed by evaluations of various kinds on the committee's ability to make decisions.

Based on the notion of evaluative expression given above, the following constructions are typical of simple claims:

1) If the main verb of the claim has a clear positive or negative polarity (e.g. *to protect, to prevent, to pollute*), then language realizations of a claim include:

(1a) a proposition with this verb,

(1b) the negation of the verb or verb phrase (VP),

(1c) the use of adverbs of frequency, completion, etc., possibly combined with a negation: *in general, almost never, seldom, rarely, not frequently, very frequently, fully, systematically*, or

(1d) the use of modals expressing doubt or uncertainty: *seem, could, should*.

For example:

> *Vaccination prevents Ebola dissemination.*
> *Vaccination does not prevent any disease dissemination.*
> *In general, vaccination should prevent disease dissemination.*

2) If the evaluative expression applies to the head noun of the claim, in general, the subject, then language realizations involve attribute structures with one or more adjectives with a clear polarity in the context at stake that evaluate the concept: *toxic, useless, expensive* or their negative forms. These can be modified by intensifiers such as: *100%, totally*. These intensifiers can also generate by themselves a debatable character proper to claims. The main verb is often neutral such as *to be* or a light verb. For example, in:

> *Women's rights are not totally respected in this part of the world.*

"not totally respected" applied to the noun "rights" introduces potential controversies.

Control constructions, where head verbs subcategorize for a proposition or a sentential complement, may transform a statement into a claim by introducing some form of uncertainty. These control constructions may also appear in supports or attacks. In both cases, their scope is the claim or the entire argument. As far as claims are concerned, control constructions can be organized according to the following linguistic categories:

– Propositional attitude verbs and expressions that express a position. In this class, verbs are included and expressions such as:

> *think, believe, I am convinced that.*

The semantics of these verbs is investigated in depth in [WIE 87]. Propositional attitude constructions can be modified by a negation or by a modal such as *would, could, have to* as in: *I would think that, I have to believe that.*

– Psychological expressions or expressions denoting a position or an experience. They include verbs and expressions such as:

> *I feel, I am worried about, I am intrigued by, dream of, be encouraged by, tend to.*

These terms are often in an initial position with respect to the statement they introduce, or in a final position for constructions such as *worries me* as in:

> *the obligation of vaccination worries me,*

where the nominalized sentence is raised to be the main focus of the sentence, it then becomes the grammatical subject.

– Performative verbs, which partly overlap with the other classes presented here. They clearly introduce the idea of a thesis or of a position that could be attacked.

Verbs in this category are, for example, *pretend, support, recommend, assume* and *claim*. Their corresponding nominal expressions are, for example, *my position, thesis* and *recommendation is*. These cues explicitly indicate that the statement they subcategorize is a claim.

– Report verbs and associated constructions. They introduce claims in a direct manner or as a reported speech from, for example, other participants in a debate or from external persons, frequently considered as experts. Similarly to the above categories, these constructions can be modified by a negation or a modal. In this category, we include verbs and expressions such as *report, say, mention, state, announce, discuss* and *claim* and their morphological variants. For some of these verbs, it is not straightforward to transform a factual statement into a claim since they do not lend themselves easily to controversies, this is the case for *report, say, announce* and *declare*, which are rather neutral and need additional linguistic cues. Conversely, terms such as *claim, affirm, maintain* and *allege* are much more typical of claims and easily induce debates. The first utterance below is not as typical of a claim as the second one, in spite of the evaluative "dangerous":

> *A doctor said that Ebola is a dangerous disease.*
> *A doctor claimed that Ebola is a dangerous disease.*

– Epistemic verbs and constructions. These also occur quite frequently. They include expressions such as:

> *know, my understanding is that, I am convinced that, I suppose, I realize, it is reasonable to assume, infer, imply, I can see, it is reasonable to, this can mean, this may mean.*

These mainly introduce doubts while others are clear positive statements.

– Modal expressions. These are left-adjuncts to a proposition that modify some of the expressions described above. Most of them either weaken the statement or introduce a hypothesis:

> *it should be possible, it is probable that.*

For example, the following claim and its justification:

> *it should be possible to have a systematic vaccination that creates sanitary belts to avoid the proliferation of the disease.*

lend themselves to debates and controversies.

– Adverbials related to the expression of opinion. They indicate the strength of a claim but also its debatable character. They include:

> *probably, necessarily, most definitely, definitely, surely, usually, frequently, often, certainly, obviously, generally speaking, of course, indeed.*

Finally, given a statement that is factual, a number of discourse structures adjoined to that fact may introduce a debatable character such as illustrations. It is not possible to develop in this section a systematic analysis of these discourse structures, however, a few relevant examples can be outlined to show the importance of this phenomenon.

Illustrations often take the form of an enumeration of elements to serve as examples. As a result, illustrations introduce some plausibility for supports or attacks because the elements in the enumeration can be used as starting points for these supports or attacks. For example:

> *the Ebola vaccine is easy to use for emerging countries (cheap, can be transported without any need for refrigeration, active for a long time).*

Even if the main claim is consensual, some of the elements of the enumeration can be subject to debates, in particular when they contain fuzzy lexical items or expressions, such as *for a long time*. The term "cheap" could also be discussed.

Claims that include a purpose or goal may be subject to debates not on the main content of the claim but on its purpose. In:

> *Vaccination against Ebola is necessary to avoid any disease proliferation in territories close to those where Ebola is present.*

the purpose can be debated in particular on the forms and speed of proliferation. Here, the purpose plays the role of a justification of the main claim. It can be attacked without really questioning the necessity of the vaccination, because it is not a very relevant justification or because it is rather weak. Similarly, the following purpose may weaken a factual statement:

> [*purpose* *in order to avoid any form of panic or, worse, of bio-terrorism*], *the authorities of Guinea closed their borders.*

For example, the permeability of the border can be outlined and discussed.

3.2. The linguistics of justifications

Identifying justifications to a claim is also very challenging both from a linguistic and conceptual point of view, in particular when justifications are not adjacent to the claim. In this section, we consider justifications to a claim C (supports) as well as justifications to its negation $\neg C$, which are attacks of C.

The first difficulty is to relate a potential justification to a claim. A justification may support a facet of a claim instead of the whole claim. The terms used in a justification may require inferences and knowledge to relate it to a claim because the linguistic, conceptual and referential links to that issue are rarely direct and explicit. This is one of the main challenges of argument mining. Justifications are often evaluative natural language statements that become justifications because of the specific relations they have with another evaluative statement considered as a claim. Besides their evaluative dimensions, justifications may be causally related to a claim.

Let us illustrate the need for knowledge and inference when relating a claim and one of its justifications with the following example:

Claim: *The situation of women has improved in India*,
Statement found in another text: (a) *early in the morning, we now see long lines of happy young girls with school bags walking along the roads*.

(a) is a justification (support) of the claim, but it requires knowledge and inferences to make explicit, and possibly explain, the relationships between women's conditions and young girls carrying school bags. Here, the relationship is education. Let us now consider:

(b) *School buses must be provided so that schoolchildren do not reach the school totally exhausted after a long early morning walk.*

(b) is an attack of (a), indeed: *these young girls may not be so happy to be walking in the early morning*, but it is not an attack of the claim: the facet that is concerned in the relation between (b) and (a) does not concern women's conditions in particular.

So far, the relatedness problem has not been addressed in depth in argument mining, although it is crucial to identify arguments. In Chapter 4, we develop a few examples that show the complexity of the problem, which is a major limitation to the development of argument mining technology.

The next difficulty is identifying that the statement that is related to a given claim is a justification. The term justification must be considered in a broad sense: a justification adds content that contributes to the acceptability of a claim. It makes the claim more plausible, but it does not prove that it is true. For example, a statement that is a reformulation or an elaboration of a claim is not a justification, since the content that is added simply makes the claim clearer or more precise. An illustration can be considered as a justification in some contexts:

Claim: *Vaccination against Ebola is dangerous*,
illustration: *One person died after an injection in Monrovia and two patients got sick in Guinea last week.*

The illustration does not really justify why the vaccination is dangerous, it however adds strength to the claim.

When a justification is adjacent to a claim or adjacent to a referential expression associated with that claim, it may be linked to that claim by means of different types of connectors, among which:

– causal connectors such as *because, since, as, so that, due to, resulting in*

– purpose connectors and expressions such as *to, in order to, so as to, to avoid, to prevent* can also be used to introduce supports as well as attacks,

– connectors and expressions describing a result may also introduce a justification, for example: *thus, therefore, as a consequence, hence, as a result,*

– illustrations may play the role of justifications: they are introduced by typical terms such as: *for example, e.g., for instance, such as, like, including,*

– weak or strong forms of attacks can be characterized by concessive connectors such as: *although, though, even if, despite, in spite of, however, nonetheless, nevertheless*, or by

– contrast connectors such as: *while, whereas, but, in contrast of, yet, instead of, rather, unlike.*

More details can be found in [ANS 83] where a large number of connectors with an argumentative orientation are presented and illustrated for French. An equivalent set can be developed for English. This investigation considers that argumentation is essentially a linguistic and language act rather than a discursive action. Claim–justification pairs are investigated from the perspective of their possible sequences in language.

Let us come back to justifications. Since they support claims, justifications are also evaluative expressions. Similarly, attacks support the negation of the claim at stake. They use some of the linguistic categories presented above for claims, in particular scalar adjectives, adverbs, verbs with a positive or negative polarity, report verbs, epistemic constructions and adverbials. The class of propositional attitude verbs is extended to take into account verbs that denote forms of acceptance of rejection such as:

> *agree, deny, argue, refute, acknowledge, reckon, disagree, accept, reject,*

possibly combined with modals such as *would*, negation or temporal or frequency adverbs: *I always disagree with...*

3.3. Evaluating the strength of claims, justifications and arguments

In an argument it is of much interest to evaluate the strength of a claim and the strength of a support or an attack separately. Strong claims call in general for stronger forms of supports or attacks than claims of a moderate strength. Therefore, the strength of a claim or of a support or an attack can be evaluated separately. Then the evaluation of a support or of an attack must be tuned with respect to the *a priori* strength of the claim to determine the overall strength of an argument.

We view the strength of a claim, a justification or an argument as a kind of metrics, which is essentially induced by linguistic factors, even if an accurate measure of the strength of a number of linguistic cues is domain dependent and difficult to evaluate. It follows that persuasion is a more pragmatic measure of strength where personal and contextual factors play an important role. These factors include readers' or listeners' profiles and expectations as well as their global cultural environment. In this chapter, strength is viewed as a linguistic phenomenon. However, strength may also be determined by other factors such as images, gestures, mimics and intonation in interactive situations (see Chapter 9).

There are several ways to measure the strength of arguments. Strength can be measured from a logical and pragmatic perspective or it can be measured from a linguistic point of view. Both approaches are not necessarily coherent but they must be combined to produce a relatively accurate measure of strength. Argument strength may be measured for each argument in isolation or for groups of related arguments, taking into account their relations and structure.

Investigations on argument strength share some aspects with the evaluation of strength in opinion analysis. This latter area is well developed and a number of resources are freely available. We do not go into it in this book. However, the notion of strength in argument mining is more complex since it involves a number of specific features, including the impact of argument schemes.

So far, investigations on argument strength have focused on a few aspects such as (1) teaching how to organize written essays and how to organize arguments and give them an appropriate strength, (2) research on persuasion which is, in our view, an analysis of strength in contexts (the domain and the audience of the argumentation are taken into account) and (3) in theoretical analysis of argumentation where graphs of attacks and supports are developed. Let us note for example [GRA 11] that deals with an in-depth analysis of persuasion and [ZHA 11] which investigates the content of persuasive messages. Sensitivity to argument strength of various populations is developed in [COR 04]. The impact of strength in conjunction with rhetorical questions has been addressed in [MUN 88]. A number of linguistic factors are analyzed in [ANS 83], and later in [EEM 01] and [EEM 92]. The notion of strength is an important element in opinion analysis, for example, to measure whether a specific feature in a product is appreciated or not, and to what extent. A number of resources has been developed to evaluate strength, in general out of context. Let us note the Stanford Sentiment Treebank (https://nlp.stanford.edu/sentiment/treebank.html). This resource is a well-developed and stable resource frequently used in opinion analysis. However, to the best of our knowledge, little has been done to characterize argument strength from a linguistic point of view and from the perspective of argument mining.

This section is organized as follows. In the first section, the contribution of individual lexical items found in propositions P_i is investigated. The hypothesis is that such propositions have an intrinsic strength independently of any claim. Next, we introduce structures from lexical semantics that enable the organization of the linguistic data. Then, the strength variations induced by the combination of several lexical items in a proposition and the support construction in which it may be embedded are explored and tested experimentally. Since it turns out that contextual effects in their broad sense are crucial to have an accurate estimate of the strength of an argument, several contextual parameters are discussed, in particular the impact of the discourse structures that are adjoined to a statement and the kind of argument scheme on which the argument relies.

3.3.1. *Strength factors within a proposition*

Similarly to the results obtained in opinion analysis, evaluating strength entailed by linguistic cues in argument expression is quite subjective. Two levels of the expression of strength are considered here: (1) the intrinsic strength conveyed by head terms used in propositions P_i and (2) the strength conveyed by expressions, such as propositional attitudes expressions, of which P_i is the sentential complement. The propositions P_i considered in this investigation have a simple syntactic structure. They are composed of a main point called the kernel and adjuncts – usually discourse structures – which add restrictions, justifications, purposes or illustrations to the kernel. These discourse structures may scope either over the proposition or over the entire argument.

There are many elements that may have an impact on the strength of a proposition P_i. Those with a higher impact are head elements such as verbs but also elements that are less prominent in the syntax such as evaluative adjectives and adverbs. The latter are analyzed as modifiers to the noun for adjectives and to the VP or to the sentence for adverbs. These linguistic elements are used to determine the orientation of the propositions P_i with respect to the claim (support, attack, possibly neutral). In addition, their implicit semantics is an important factor to evaluate the overall strength of an argument.

A number of categories of lexical items are developed below, some are shared with opinion analysis or sentiment analysis while others are more specific to argument analysis.

The main categories of elements internal to a proposition P_i that contribute to strength expression are as follows:

1) Positively oriented verbs, such as:

improve, benefit, optimize, reinforce, preserve, strengthen, guarantee, consolidate.

e.g. *vaccination against Ebola is necessary because it guarantees the non-proliferation of the disease.*

There are many such verbs. Their exact semantic contribution to strength and their orientation may depend on domains.

2) Negatively oriented verbs, such as:

affect, alter, break, demolish, hurt, lessen, ruin, undermine, damage.

For example, the claim:

the situation of women in India has improved,

is attacked by the proposition:

the persistent lack of education largely undermines their independence.

3) Similarly to verbs, a number of adjectives and adjectival compounds contribute to the orientation of an argument and the expression of strength. These are usually found in propositions where the verb is neutral (auxiliary, light verb, verbs such as *allow, enable*, where the orientation of the object is crucial) or where the verb is largely underspecified with respect to polarity and strength. Adjectives in this category are, for example:

useful, capable, consistent, resistant, compliant, beneficial, optimal

for the positively oriented ones and:

risky, polluted, dangerous, weak, harmful

for the negatively oriented ones. A typical example is:

vaccination against Ebola is dangerous because the adjuvant is toxic,

where *toxic* induces the orientation and the strength.

4) Expressions derived from verbs, past participles and adjectival compounds with a scalar dimension such as:

disappointing, potentially risky.

For example, a negatively oriented argument in relation with a standpoint on the necessity of nuclear plants is:

Pipe corrosion in nuclear plants is potentially risky.

5) Nouns that appear as subjects or objects in the proposition that have a positive or negative orientation, e.g. *risk, disease, reward* and *success.*

The expression of strength is also mediated by a number of terms, which introduce supports or attacks. These are called *control constructions*. These are composed of head verbs that subcategorize for a proposition or a sentential complement. Their scope is therefore the entire argument.

Control constructions can be organized according to several linguistic categories, which have been presented in the above sections. They include propositional attitude verbs, psychological expressions, report verbs, some epistemic constructions and modal expressions. They also include adverbs and adverb phrases denoting strength, frequency or probability, for example, *probably, necessarily, most definitely, definitely, surely, usually, frequently, often, certainly, of course, obviously, generally speaking, of course* and *indeed*.

3.3.2. *Structuring expressions of strength by semantic category*

It is obviously impossible to *a priori* assign strength values to the lexical items and expressions of the different categories given above, nor is it possible to assign weights to their combinations. An option is to structure these terms along scales, as for scalar adjectives in opinion analysis. In various experiments, it turns out that the polarity of about 75% of the adjectives is stable over domains. While the adjectives used in opinion expression lend themselves relatively easily to an evaluation of their positive or negative character, this is more complex for verbs, modals or the expressions given above. To organize the elements in the different categories, an experiment is made using non-branching proportional series [CRU 86], which allow to define partial orders over groups of terms with respect to a given measurable property. These scales organize terms of a category from those with a strong negative orientation to those with a strong positive orientation. A neutral point is mentioned: it is either a lexical term when such a term exists or an abstract point. The partial order introduces some flexibility by allowing several terms to be at a given point on the scale when it is not relevant or easy to make strength distinctions between them.

For example, the negatively and positively oriented verbs can be structured as follows:

```
[[ruin] - [break, demolish] - [hurt, alter, lessen, undermine, damage] -
[affect] - Neutral - [preserve, guarantee] - [benefit] -
[improve, consolidate, strengthen] - [optimize]].
```

Terms that are considered to have almost the same strength appear in the same set, represented between square brackets. The neutral point is represented by the constant "Neutral", the two sets just before and after it have a moderate strength while the extremes sets are the strongest ones.

Adjectives are more difficult to structure because they do not modify the same property in a homogeneous way; for example, *resistant* and *optimal* do not operate on the same concepts, where *optimal* is rather of higher order. A scale that represents a kind of "safety" dimension can be developed as follows:

```
[[dangerous, harmful] - [risky, polluted] - [unsafe] - Neutral -
[useful, beneficial] - [safe] - [certified]].
```

In this example, a certain number of adjectives are in the same set since these have a relatively similar impact on strength.

Finally, here is a scale for propositional attitude verbs:

```
[[deny - refute - reject] - [disagree] - Neutral -
[believe, think, accept] - [agree, acknowledge, reckon] - [argue]].
```

The verbs to the extreme sides of the scale are more crucial in the acceptance or rejection of the claim than those close to the neutral point. Adverbials modify these verbs or the corresponding VP by adding or reducing the strength. These can be classified as follows by increasing levels of strength:

```
[[probably] - [indeed, usually, of course] -
[often, frequently, generally speaking] -
[definitely, surely, obviously, necessarily] - [most definitely]].
```

This approach can be extended to other categories of terms, which play a role in strength expression.

3.3.3. *A simple representation of strength when combining several factors*

It is frequent to have supports or attacks that include several terms expressing strength. For example, given the claim:

Nuclear plants are useful since they pollute less than coal or oil.

a proposition such as:

I am definitely convinced that nuclear plants should be banished.

includes the strong negative term *banished* in its statement, which is somewhat softened by the modal *should*. This proposition is included into an epistemic construction with a strong connotation: a strong verb *convinced* modified by the intensifier adverb *definitely*. Evaluating the strength of such a proposition compared to:

I am convinced that nuclear plants must be banished.

is not trivial, even for human experts.

To have an accurate analysis of the strength of propositions, a semantic representation of the elements that contribute to strength expression can be developed and interpreted via an interpretation model, which is largely experimental. This model is based on the categories of the elements found in the proposition and on a rough estimate of their strength, as reflected by the non-branching proportional series presented in section 3.3.2. For example, the proposition:

Nuclear plants should be banished.

has the following semantic representation with respect to its strength:

$[_{argument}$ verb(strong negative) $\wedge$ modal(weaken)$]$ where head terms have an attribute that represents their strength and modals or adverbials include an attribute that describes their function on the term they modify. In this example, *banished* is among the strongest negative verbs on the corresponding scale while the modal *should* weakens the strength of this verb. Next, the more complex proposition:

I am definitely convinced that nuclear plants should be banished,

which includes an epistemic construction, is represented as follows:

$[_{control}$ verb(epistemic, strong positive) $\wedge$ adverbial(reinforce)$]$ $([_{argument}$ verb(strong negative) $\wedge$ modal(weaken)$]$).

Let us call this expression the *signature of the strength of the proposition*. Considering the different elements of this representation, the resulting strength is strong with a negative orientation. It would however be necessary to develop more accurate models based on readers' real perception of strength, possibly via learning methods from specific annotations.

3.3.4. *Pragmatic factors of strength expression*

Several other factors, which are essentially contextual, have a major influence on the strength of supports or attacks, and on arguments more generally. Their influence is however difficult to accurately analyze.

The first factor is the discourse structures that may be adjoined to a proposition or to an argument. They mainly develop circumstances, conditions, restrictions and elaborations. The second factor is the argument scheme that has been used. Some are more commonly admitted or closer to deduction and are therefore stronger than others. The third factor is the context of the proposition interpreted as a support or an attack: it may be uttered in isolation or it may be part of a series of propositions. As developed in [EEM 92], propositions associated with a claim may be structured by series or in parallel. In the first case, the strength is the strength of the weakest one, and in the second case it is the strength of the strongest one. The fourth factor is the syntactic structure of the premise–conclusion pair where focus shifts can be observed via left extraposition. The last factor is the linguistic context of the utterance. For example, some debates may only use soft arguments in order to remain polite and to avoid strong attacks, whereas others use extremely strong terms even for arguments that are not crucial. In this section, the impact on argument strength of the first two factors is discussed. The remaining ones require additional investigations.

3.3.4.1. *Influence of discourse structures on argument strength*

Arguments are quite frequently associated with elements such as comments, elaborations, comparisons and illustrations, which can be considered as either forms of explanation or secondary or subordinated arguments. Some examples are developed in section 3.1 of this chapter. Let us consider here more complex cases, frequently encountered in argumentation related to opinion analysis. The discourse analysis provided here has been carried out with the discourse analysis platform TextCoop [SAI 12] (see also section 7.3.9).

The role of illustrations with respect to argument strength may be complex. Given the claim:

I do not recommend this hotel,

and a proposition such as:

The bathrooms were in bad condition: $[_{ILLUSTRATION}$ *the showers leaked, and the plug mechanism in the bath jammed ...],*

the illustrations given to support the diagnosis ("bad condition'") do not seem to reinforce or weaken its strength. These are interpreted as reformulations, which is another way to say something without altering the initial content.

Let us consider other types of discourse relations such as the *circumstance* and *justification relations*. For example, possibly with a form of irony, the strength and polarity of "breakfast is excellent" is largely affected – if not reversed – by the contrast:

The breakfast is excellent,

$[_{PRECISION}$ *with very imaginative exotic fruit salads*]
$[_{CONTRAST}$ *but most of the products are not fresh and most have passed their sell-by date*].

More complex – yet realistic – arguments associated with restrictions of various sorts make the identification of the overall strength of an argument and of its various components quite challenging:

$[_{CONTEXT}$ *We stayed here for a one day conference off-season],
and the hotel was OK*
$[_{CONCESSION}$ *- although the room I had was kind of weird.*]
I think it was the sitting room to the suite on the top floor

[*PRECISION* - *the bed was a fold-out bed, not comfortable,* [*CONCESSION* (*slept okay though*)], *and the coffee table was small, dirty and pushed to the side.*]
[*CONCESSION* It did have a lovely terrace though] - *shame it was raining cats and dogs.*
[*RECOMMENDATION* Not a great experience.]

Depending on customers' preferences, this opinion can be judged to be slightly positive or negative, in spite of the negative polarity of the recommendation, which turns out to be the main claim. Therefore, this opinion may either support or attack the claim *I do not recommend this hotel.*

Evaluating the impact of discourse structures is therefore a very challenging task. Even if the polarity and strength of each individual structure can be evaluated, their combination with the main argument and their interactions when there are several structures is complex and highly domain dependent.

3.3.4.2. *The impact of argument schemes on argument strength*

Another component that has an impact on strength is the inner structure of an argument and the underlying scheme that has been used. [WAL 08, WAL 15a, PAR 08] have identified and structured a large number of schemes which are used in everyday argumentation. Some of them can be detected via a linguistic analysis [FEN 11, GRE 17]. These can provide information on the strength of arguments. A number of schemes among the most frequently encountered are reviewed in this section; they complement the schemes presented in section 2.5.2.

– Argument from analogy

The typical form of arguments from analogy is as follows:

Premise 1: Generally, case C1 is similar to case C2.

Premise 2: A is true (false) in case C1.

Conclusion: A is true (false) in case C2.

For example:

> *It has been shown that vaccinating against malaria can be useless in some cases; similarly, the vaccine against Ebola is not recommended.*

This sentence makes an analogy between two serious diseases and tries to show that if the vaccine against one of these diseases is useless, then the vaccine against the other is useless too. Some linguistic cues marking analogy are: *similarly, x is like y, doing x is as [adjective useful, dangerous, crucial] as doing y.*

– Argument from expert opinion

The typical structure of arguments from expert opinion is:

Premise 1: E is a reliable authority in the domain S.

Premise 2: A is a proposition contained in S.

Premise 3: E asserts that A.

Conclusion: Therefore, A.

An example of argument from expert opinion is :

> *Depression and anxiety should be taken seriously. The London School of Economy reports that half of all illnesses in the under 65s is mental.*

Arguments from expert opinion are marked by two linguistic cues; first, nouns that identify the expert by his title or his function (e.g. *expert, doctor, economist* and *politician*); second, constructions such as reported speech that allow to indicate the expert's opinion (e.g. *claim, warn, explain* and *indicate*). The strength of report verbs must be taken into account in the scheme. The opinion of experts is used in many cases to support a claim since it is hard to contradict an expertise. As a result, arguments from expert opinion have a strong impact.

– Argument from negative consequences

This scheme has the following form:

Premise 1: If an action leads to bad consequences, all else being equal, it should not be brought about.

Premise 2: If action A is brought about, bad consequences will occur.

Conclusion: Therefore, A should not be brought about.

For example:

> *Vaccinating people against Ebola has reduced their immune system. This vaccine must not be used anymore.*

is an argument from negative consequences.

Negative adjectives, nouns or verbs are usually found in the premise(s) (here, *reduce*), while action verbs used in the negative form are used in the conclusion (here, *must not be used*). Warning against negative consequences can have a strong impact, but the nouns and adjectives used can help determining how strong the argument is.

– Arguments from examples

This scheme has the following form:

Premise 1: Example 1 is an example that supports claim P.

Premise 2: Example n is an example that supports claim P.

Conclusion: Claim P is true.

An illustration is:

> *It has been shown that the vaccine is not the right solution. For example, two weeks after the injection, an old man died and the fetus of a pregnant woman showed malformations.*

Linguistic cues typical of illustration such as *for example, for instance, in the same manner* can contribute to detect arguments from example. Evaluating how the strength induced by this scheme interacts with the strength induced by the other argument schemes presented above requires some experimentation. It is not clear, for example, if they all operate at the same level, or if some have a higher weight. The strength of the argument based on examples can be measured from the number of examples used. The above argument has two premises (two examples) supporting the claim. The conclusion could be supported by many other examples of people who reacted badly to the vaccine, which would reinforce the claim that the vaccine is not the right solution.

– Arguments from position to know

This scheme has the following form:

Premise 1: Source a is in a position to know about things in a certain subject domain S containing proposition A.

Premise 2: a asserts that A (in Domain S) is true (false).

Conclusion: A is true (false).

An illustration is:

> *A British politician visiting Western Africa has revealed that the number of deaths due to Ebola has dropped since the vaccination began. Vaccinating populations must therefore continue.*

In this example, the claim that vaccinating against Ebola must continue is supported by the opinion of a British political figure. This type of argument is close to arguments from expert opinion. However, arguments from position to know are weaker than arguments from expert opinion because it is easier to question whether the person is able to have a clear and well-established opinion on that topic.

– Argument from popular opinion

Arguments from popular opinion take the following form:

Premise 1: Everybody is doing X.

Premise 2: X is a good thing to do.

Conclusions: Therefore, X must be the right thing to do.

An illustration is:

> *vaccination in general is a cheap and efficient way to get rid of major diseases, therefore all populations exposed to Ebola must systematically undergo vaccination.*

Linguistic cues referring to populations and groups of people can help detect arguments from popular opinion (e.g. *the population, people, individuals, everyone* and *all the persons*). Similarly to arguments from position to know, arguments from popular opinion have less strength than the ones from expert opinion since the actions or opinions of groups of people can be discussed.

– Arguments from cause to effect

This scheme has the following form:

Premise 1: Doing X will cause Y to occur or If X occurs then Y will occur,

Premise 2: X is done or X occurs,

Conclusion: Y will occur.

The statement:

> *A new vaccine has been developed, which will lower the number of deaths. Fewer farmers in the vaccinated area will die after its injection.*

is an example of argument from cause to effect. This type of argument can be seen as an anticipation. Anticipation has, however, little credibility in many cases and, as a result, arguments from cause to effect are in general weak arguments.

– Organizing schemes with respect to their strength

From the observations above, and as an illustration, a tentative classification of argument strength induced by argument schemes can be made. No domain knowledge is considered in this classification:

Strong: analogy, expert opinion

Moderate: negative consequences, from examples

Weak: position to know, popular opinion, cause to effect.

In [WAL 08], each scheme is associated with a number of critical questions that allow testing the soundness of the argument; these can be used in particular to attack the argument. For instance, the argument from analogy has the following critical questions:

– Are there respects in which C1 and C2 are different that would tend to undermine the force of the similarity cited?

– Is A the right conclusion to be drawn in C1?

– Is there some other case C3 that is also similar to C1, but in which some conclusion other than A could be drawn?

Additional examples of critical questions are provided in Chapter 2.

Evaluating the overall strength of critical questions per scheme can be used to determine the strength of the scheme with respect to an argument. An argument that has stronger critical questions could be a weak argument (it can be easily attacked), or, on the contrary, it can be a strong one (it is difficult to defeat it) if it does not raise so many critical questions.

Finally, the problem of fallacious arguments can interfere with strength evaluation. For example, analogy is sometimes classified as fallacious. Evaluating fallacious arguments is a major concern in argumentation, however, in practical situations, this means considering domain and general purpose knowledge and inferences that are beyond the current state of the art of argument mining.

3.4. Rhetoric and argumentation

Rhetoric is an important component of argumentation and vice versa. Rhetoric, from a linguistic point of view, has developed models to organize claim justifications, argument supports and attacks in a structured way with the goal of being as efficient and convincing as possible. Planning issues are essential in rhetoric. For example, starting with the less prominent justifications and ending with the most crucial ones with which almost everybody agrees is a frequent strategy to convince an audience. This planning activity may also anticipate attacks from opponents by presenting them and refuting them. Rhetoric also deals with linguistic aspects such as lexical choice and syntactic structure. Finally, rhetoric offers a unified view of linguistic expression paired with non-verbal means such as gestures, mimics, various forms of sounds and images. Rhetoric is therefore a major component of argumentation in real contexts. In this section, the main features of rhetoric are introduced. There is an important literature on rhetoric, starting from [PER 58].

3.4.1. *Rhetoric and communication*

Rhetoric, as well as argumentation, is based on the following three main communication paradigms:

– demonstration: which develops an impersonal mode. It uses facts, axioms and inference rules. There are various types of logics and forms of demonstrations, whose goal is to identify whether a statement is true or false;

– dialectic: which is the art of dialog. Dialectic does not deal with truth, but with what is probable. However, it uses rigorous protocols, norms and forms of reasoning to reach the best consensus on a topic. Dialectic uses argumentation in situations such as debates, negotiation or mediation;

– sophism: which is typically the area of duplicity and cheating. It is based on false assumptions that, nevertheless, seem plausible to an audience.

The ideal model of an argumentation is organized as follows:

1) confrontation stage: recognition of a difference of opinion on a certain topic that is made explicit and unambiguous;

2) opening stage: decision to try to resolve the issue following a number of argumentation and cooperativity rules (Chapter 2) on which the different parties agree;

3) argumentation stage: defense of standpoints via argumentation rules, argumentation schemes and conventions. This stage uses facts to develop justifications;

4) conclusion stage: assessment of the differences or agreement on a compromise.

In these stages, argumentation and explanation may co-exist in order, for example, to bring new information to the opponent or to change his/her beliefs.

The main features claimed and developed by rhetoric to be crucial in any argumentation process can be summarized as follows:

– language appropriateness and correctness: these requirements concern, in particular, lexical choice, the syntax of utterances, the use of an appropriate genre, for example, judicial, deliberative, epidictic (to make the panegyric of someone). At a more global level, features related to style such as being clear (no ambiguity), being pleasant to listen or to read (metaphors, figures of speech), being well illustrated, etc. are also crucial to build a convincing argumentation.

– appropriate level of style depending on the situation and the audience: simple (based on *logos* and proofs), middle (based on *ethos* with the goal to give a good impression to the audience) and noble (based on *pathos*), which is mainly used for persuasion or in special circumstances.

– use of appropriate figures of speech, which concern words (play on words for effects), construction (e.g. ellipsis), meaning (metaphors), thought (develops the relation between the orator, its topic, and the discourse using forms of irony or emphasis, for example).

The remainder of this section develops the main features of rhetoric: logos, ethos and pathos and their conceptual, communication and linguistic features.

3.4.2. *Logos: the art of reasoning and of constructing demonstrations*

Logos is the most rational component of rhetoric. It introduces deduction and reasoning into a discourse that is not necessarily very rational. The motivation is that some forms of logical reasoning are often necessary to establish controversies. There are several strategies to develop an argumentation. They depend on the profile of the audience and on the difficulty to justify the claim at stake. The development of an appropriate plan to deliver justifications is crucial. Such plans are a matter of experience rather than the use of preestablished, ready-made plans. Content planning and defining the macrostructure of a text or an oral presentation is a topic that has been addressed in length in natural language generation (NLG).

The main linguistic features of logos are the argumentative value of negation and negative expressions, the impact of interrogative forms, in particular the use of rhetorical questions, the syntactic forms which are used and in particular the use of left-extraposition (moving constituents to the left in a sentence) to create focus effects, the use of reported speech and citations to refer to different types of authors (e.g. to develop arguments from authority), the use of modals, etc.

The impact of lexical choice is very important in an argumentative discourse. The weight of an argument may depend on the terms that are used because of their ease of understanding and familiarity for an audience, their potential connotations, for example, the opposition between the terms *wild* and *uncontrolled*, the induced irony or their *a priori* polarity. For example, systematically using positively oriented terms, even in a context with high controversies may shed a positive light on the discourse even if this positive character is not totally motivated. In the same range of ideas, lexical re-interpretations and semantic variations (e.g. *war* instead of *conflict of interest* or *men who fight with each other* may radically change perspectives).

Besides the purely linguistic aspects, the logos aspect includes conceptual aspects, in particular:

– the development of implicit aspects in the reasoning and planning process. The goal is to leave the opponents to make their own inferences. This often induces an argumentation with fewer possibilities for debate: what is implicit is indeed viewed as obvious. The listeners or opponents probably agree with it or make their own inferences concerning what is left implicit. It is important for the orator to have a good analysis of the shared knowledge and beliefs of their opponents in order to use them as much as possible;

– the use of presuppositions, which can often be reconstructed linguistically. This approach is more objective than using implicit elements, however, it has a stronger persuasion effect. Implicit elements can be reconstructed via Grice's implicature system, when presuppositions obey cooperation maxims. This system is useful to reconstruct the missing premises of an argumentation;

– the use of appropriate connectors that bind two explicit statements. The most frequently encountered connectors are *but, however, because, notwithstanding, nevertheless*. Each of them is used in a specific context: they indeed have their own pragmatic profile and implications.

3.4.3. *Ethos: the orator profile*

Ethos is a crucial component in dialogues and debates. It mainly deals with the communication parameters of the orator, in particular his/her behavior (e.g. listens to the audience, is cheerful), his/her personality (e.g. attractive, happy, optimistic), how s/he speaks (e.g. in a fluid manner, with hesitation, with the help of notes), how s/he is dressed, what kind of facial expressions are used, possibly her/his environment (lights, scenery), whether s/he is sitting or standing up, etc.

Ethos is a major parameter of strength and persuasion. The goal of ethos is to develop emotion and seduction to gain the empathy of the opponent(s) or of the audience. To reach this goal, ethos stimulates the listeners' imagination, while taking into account, as much as possible, their desires and expectations. Another feature, which reinforces the stability and the veracity of the arguments, is to adhere as much as possible to the doxa, i.e. what is commonly admitted, even if it is debatable.

To reach this goal, the speaker must have a good analysis of the expectations of his audience and of the psychological profile of his opponent(s) to behave correctly and to follow the audience expectations. There are many examples, for example in advertising, where nice web pages are developed to make readers dream, with a focus on their desires.

From a linguistic point of view, ethos is also concerned with lexical choice aspects and the syntax of sentences. These linguistic elements closely interact with non-verbal elements such as gestures, jokes and metaphors. Doxa is marked by specific marks such as *it has always been the case, as we all know* and *we all agree that P is true*. In some cases, rhetorical questions can also be used to mark doxa.

3.4.4. *Pathos: how to persuade an audience*

Pathos is the art of persuading an audience and of touching the opponent. It is the audience dimension of rhetoric, this complements the features of ethos, but these two aspects of rhetoric are closely related.

The first characteristic of pathos is the way the orator acts on an audience or on her/his opponents. The main elements deployed by pathos is how to touch an audience, make it become angry, frightened or, conversely, make it happy, feel safe or confident. The orator must care not to make confusions with her/his own emotions. Pathos is not necessarily a very honest and transparent process. It uses two opposite facets: to convince (rational component of the audience) and to persuade (irrational component). Pathos is based on the fact that emotions are also value judgments of a high strength in a cognitive perspective. Emotions can then be "argued".

One of the major risks is that pathos, via its persuasion effects, deeply affects the rationality (logos) of the argumentation. The risk then is that the audience develops a feeling of trickery. There are a few linguistic cues which are typical of trickery, lies and audience manipulation. They are characterized by the use of repetitions and terms that develop insistence such as *really, completely, definitely, absolutely, totally* and *truthful*. These also insist on the truthfulness of statements, which are not necessarily true.

Pathos makes a systematic use of *ad hominen* and *ad populum* argument schemes to attack opponents and discredit them. This strategy deeply affects the overall quality of logos. Pathos must be paired with references to moral values to get all of its impact and power. These values may depend on the argumentation context. In situations such as debates, negotiation, mediation and warning of a danger (*ad baculum*), values may be quite different.

In conceptual terms, pathos develops emotions that are frequently in relation with the audience's preferred images, topics and beliefs (e.g. children = innocence) or major social schemes. The challenge is that the same images can produce very different emotions depending on how they are presented in an argumentation and how emotion is constructed. Similarly, the rejection of emotions can be a positive strategy in an argumentation, even if this rejection is artificial or fake. This is realized by means of typical terms that reverse the polarity of the arguments. Emotion is lexicalized with specific linguistic and pragmatic marks. Other elements typical of emotion expression include style, emphasis, rhythm and repetitions.

4

Advanced Features of Argumentation for Argument Mining

This chapter addresses a few complex challenges for argument mining and for argumentation more generally. It is not crucial to develop a simple argument mining system. It should however draw the attention of the reader interested in undertaking some research in this area.

In this chapter, we first develop a few tricky situations where opposite claims can be supported by the same justification, and where opposite justifications can support the same claim. The aim is to show that argument mining needs to cope with complex cognitive realities. Then, we discuss two topics that are crucial in argument mining: first, the need for knowledge and inference to bind a claim with an attack or a support when they are not adjacent, and second, the need to present a synthesis of the arguments that have been mined. These may be numerous and with various forms of overlap and relevance. In that case, readability is a real challenge. In this chapter, we can only report preliminary experiments and solutions since research has not reached further at the moment.

4.1. Managing incoherent claims and justifications

Argument mining reflects the complexity of human thinking. It is possible for a justification to be given for a claim and its opposite (the two standpoints involved), while still being deemed perfectly acceptable in both cases. Conversely, contradictory justifications can be mined for a given claim.

4.1.1. *The case of justifications supporting opposite claims*

Let us first consider the case of a justification that supports two opposite claims. In opinion analysis, which is an area where argumentation is highly developed, it is possible to mine the two following arguments:

A1: This hotel is very nice because it is close to bars and cinemas.
A2: This hotel is terrible because it is close to bars and cinemas.

The claim C_2 *this hotel is terrible* contradicts the claim C_1 *this hotel is very nice* because of the adjectives "very nice" and "terrible", which are antonyms in this domain. However, these two arguments are perfectly acceptable with the same justification *close to bars and cinemas*.

If we consider again Toulmin's model given in section 2.2.1, this apparent contradiction can be justified by considering two different warrant and backing systems. Argument A1 is based, for example, on the following informally formulated warrant W_1 and backing B_1:

W_1: *it is pleasant to stay close to social and cultural activities*;
B_1: *humans generally live in a dense social context where they have a high feeling of satisfaction and fulfillment.*

A possible rebuttal R_1 can be formulated as follows:

unless the environment generates too many problems (noise, insecurity).

Argument A2 is based, for example, on the following informally formulated warrant W_2 and backing B_2 and possibly B_3 since several backings can be advocated in such a model:

W_2: *public places with bars and cinemas are very noisy, dangerous and unsafe*;
B_2: *humans generally prefer safe and stable places*;
B_3: *large human concentrations usually generate trouble and danger.*

A rebuttal can be:

R_2: *unless there is a very strict police control.*

Note however that A2 is not equivalent to A3:

This hotel is very nice because it is far from noisy places such as bars and cinemas.

The divergences between A1 and A2 can be explained in terms of value system or preferences where some warrants may have higher weights than others for specific categories of persons. Rebuttal R_1 shows restrictions that are in fact close to W_2 and B_2. It is also worth noting that the warrants and backings given here are not inconsistent: they simply relate two different facets of the situation advocated in the arguments A1 and A2.

4.1.2. *The case of opposite justifications justifying the same claim*

Two opposite justifications can support the same claim. Consider, for example:

A3: This film must be banished because it is politically incorrect
A4: This film must be banished because it is not politically incorrect.

Similarly as above, there is a divergence in warrants and backings, for example for A3 we may have, informally:

W_3: *only politically correct ideas must be developed in public*;
B_3: *the public must be educated according to moral principles.*

A rebuttal can be:

R_3: *unless the goal is to educate people by means of counterexamples.*

For A4, we may have, informally:

W_4: *it is good to criticize standard education to promote the evolution of minds*;
B_4: *in education it is crucial to develop critical thinking*;
R_4: *unless some historical aspect is developed.*

Similarly to the previous section, the warrants and backings produced for A3 and A4 are not incompatible. They correspond to different views or facets of a complex situation. Therefore, A3 and A4 are acceptable and correspond to different priorities, preferences of value systems of their utterer. A justification and its opposite may therefore support the same claim with the same strength. Extensions to Toulmin's standard model can be developed to accommodate these observations.

4.2. Relating claims and justifications: the need for knowledge and reasoning

One of the challenges in argument mining is to establish that a statement can be interpreted as justification of a given claim, in particular when these two statements are not adjacent, possibly not in the same text or dialog turn. Two conditions must be satisfied: this statement must be semantically and pragmatically related to that claim and it must formulate a position, often under the form of an evaluative expression. We report here an experimentation carried out by [SAI 16a], which shows the importance of knowledge and inferences in the analysis of relatedness.

4.2.1. *Investigating relatedness via corpus analysis*

To explore and characterize the forms of knowledge that are required to investigate the problem of relatedness in argument mining, four corpora were constructed and annotated based on four independent controversial issues. These corpora are relatively small, they are designed to explore the needs in terms of knowledge, knowledge organization and reasoning schemes. An annotation scheme is proposed to guide this identification.

For this experiment, the four following claims are considered, which involve very different types of arguments, forms of knowledge (concrete or relatively abstract) and language realizations:

1) *Ebola vaccination is necessary*;

2) *the conditions of women has improved in India*;

3) *the development of nuclear plants is necessary*;

4) *organic agriculture is the future.*

Texts were collected on the web, considering claims as web queries. The text fragments that were selected are extracted from various sources in which these claims are discussed, in particular newspaper articles and blogs from associations. These are documents accessible to a large public, with no professional consideration, they can therefore be understood by almost every reader.

A large number of texts were collected for each claim. For each text, the task was to manually identify justifications related to the claim at stake. The unit considered for justifications is the sentence. These units are tagged <argument>. As a preliminary step, all the supports and attacks related to each claim were identified. In a second stage, supports or attacks judged by the annotator to be similar or redundant were eliminated and a single utterance, judged to be the most representative in terms of content and structure, is kept. The goals of this preliminary investigation were (1) to gradually develop relevant annotation guidelines, as is the case for most argument annotation projects (see Chapter 6), (2) to evaluate the impact of knowledge in argument mining processes and (3) to suggest which forms of knowledge and inferences are needed.

For each of these issues, the corpus characteristics and the different attacks and supports found are summarized in Table 4.1. In this table, the number of words in column 2 represents the total size of the text portions that were considered for this task, i.e. paragraphs that contain at least one attack or support.

This corpus shows that the diversity of attacks and supports per claim is not very large. A relatively high overlap rate was observed: while there are original statements, authors tend to borrow quite a lot of material from each other. For example, for claim (1) an average redundancy rate of 4.7 was observed, i.e. the same statement was found 4.7 times on average in different texts. This overlap rate is somewhat subjective since it depends on the annotator's analysis and on the size of the corpus. In spite of this subjectivity, this rate gives an interesting approximate redundancy level. With a large corpus, this overlap rate would likely increase, while the number of new arguments would gradually decrease. A more detailed analysis of those repetitions would be of much interest from a rhetorical and sociological perspective.

Claim number	Corpus size	No. of different attacks or supports	Overlap rate (number of similar arguments)
(1)	16 texts, 8,300 words	50	4.7
(2)	10 texts, 4,800 words	27	4.5
(3)	7 texts, 5,800 words	31	3.3
(4)	23 texts, 6,200 words	22	3.8
Total	56 texts, 25,100 words	130	4.07

Table 4.1. *Corpus characteristics*

The last step in the analysis of the corpus consists in manually tagging the discourse structures found in those sentences identified as supports or attacks (called statements in the annotations). For that purpose, the TextCoop platform we developed [SAI 12] is used with an accuracy of about 90%, since sentences are relatively simple. Discourse structures that are identified are those usually found associated with arguments. They express conditions, circumstances, causes, goal and purpose expressions, contrasts and concessions. The goal is to identify the kernel of the statement (tagged <kernel>), which is in general the main proposition of the sentence, and its sentential modifiers. In addition, the discourse structures may give useful indications on the argumentation strategy that is used. Here is an example of the tagging, at this stage, for a statement that could be related to claim (1):

<statement>
<concession> Even if the vaccine seems 100% efficient and without any side effects on the tested population, </concession>
<kernel> it is necessary to wait for more conclusive data before making large vaccination campaigns </kernel>
<elaboration> The national authority of Guinea has approved the continuation of the tests on targeted populations.</elaboration>
</statement>.

4.2.2. A corpus analysis of the knowledge involved

The next step is to define a set of preliminary tags appropriate for analyzing the impact and the types of knowledge involved in argument mining. Discourse analysis tags are kept as described above and new tags are introduced, with the goal to identify the need for knowledge in argument mining. Tags mark the structure of the supports and attacks that have been manually identified for each claim, and include:

– the *text span involved and its identifier*, which are, respectively, a sentence and a number;

– the *discourse relations* associated with the statement being considered: these are annotated using the tags defined in the TextCoop platform as described above;

– the *polarity of the statement* with respect to the claim with one of the following values: support or attack. Weaker values such as concession or attack can also be used;

– the *strength of the statement*, which is mainly related to linguistic factors. It must be contrasted with persuasion effects that depend on the context and on the listener. It has the following values: strong, average, moderate;

– the *conceptual relation to the claim*: informal specification of why it is an attack or a support based on the terms used in the claim or in the "knowledge involved" attribute;

– the *knowledge involved*: list of the main concepts used to identify relatedness between a claim and a statement. These elements preferably come from a predefined domain ontology, or from the annotator's intuitions and personal knowledge, if no ontology is available. This list may be quite informal, but it nevertheless contributes to the characterization of the nature of the knowledge involved in identifying relatedness.

A statement that attacks issue (1) is then tagged as follows:

<statement nb= 11, polarity= attack, strength= moderate,
relationToIssue= limited proof of efficiency, limited safety of vaccination,
conceptsInvolved= efficiency measure, safety measures, evaluation methods>
<concession> Even if the vaccine seems 100% efficient and without any side effects on the tested population, </concession>
<kernel> it is necessary to wait for more conclusive data before making large vaccination campaigns </kernel>
<elaboration> The national authority of Guinea has approved the continuation of the tests on targeted populations.</elaboration>
</statement>.

Claims (1)–(4) (section 4.2.1) involve different types of analyses that show the different facets of the knowledge needs. While claims (1) and (4) involve relatively concrete and simple concepts, claim (2) is much more abstract. It involves abstract concepts related to education, the family and human rights. Finally, claim (3) involves fuzzier arguments, which are essentially comparisons with other sources of energy. This panel of claims, even if it is far from comprehensive, provides a first analysis of the types of knowledge used to characterize relatedness.

Dealing with knowledge remains a very difficult issue in general that is difficult to formally characterize. Knowledge representation is a vast area in artificial intelligence and in linguistics. This area involves a large diversity of forms, from linguistic knowledge (e.g. semantic types assigned to concepts, roles played by predicate arguments) to forms involving inferences (presuppositions, implicit data) via domain and general purpose knowledge, contextual knowledge, etc. Each of these aspects of knowledge requires different representation formalisms, with associated inferential patterns. They also often involve complex acquisition procedures. The notion of concept that is used in this section corresponds to the notion of concept in a domain ontology, where they can be either terminal (basic notions) or relational.

For the purpose of illustration, let us focus on claim (1). Arguments mainly attack or support salient features of the main concepts of the claim or closely related ones by means of various forms of evaluative expressions. Samples of supports and attacks associated with claim (1) are as follows:

Supports: vaccine protection is very good; Ebola is a dangerous disease; high contamination risks; vaccine has limited side effects; no medical alternative to vaccine, etc.;

Attacks: limited number of cases and deaths compared to other diseases; limited risks of contamination, ignorance of contamination forms; competent staff and P4 lab difficult to develop; vaccine toxicity and high rate of side effects;

Weaker forms: some side effects; high production and development costs; vaccine not yet available; ethical and personal liberties problems.

For claim (1), the term *vaccine* is the central concept. The concepts used to express supports or attacks for or against that claim can be structured as follows, from this central concept *vaccine*:

1) concepts which are *parts* of a vaccine: the *adjuvant* and the active principle. For example, a part of the vaccine, the adjuvant, is said to be toxic for humans;

2) concepts associated with vaccine *super types*: a vaccine is a type of or an instance of the concept medicine; it therefore inherits the properties of "medicine" (e.g. an argument says the vaccine has a high rate of side effects) unless property inheritance is blocked;

3) concepts that describe the *purposes, functions, goals and consequences* of a vaccine, and how it is *created*, i.e. developed, tested and sold. These concepts are the most frequently advocated in arguments for or against issue (1). For example, the concept of *contamination* is related to one of the purposes of a vaccine, namely to avoid that other people get the disease via contamination, and therefore on a larger scale, the purpose of a vaccine is to prevent *disease dissemination*. Finally, *production costs* are related to the creation and development of any product, including medicines and vaccines.

Without knowing that a vaccine protects humans from getting a disease, it is not possible, for example, to say that *prevents high contamination risks* is a support for claim (1) and to explain why. Similarly, without knowing that the active principle of a vaccine is diluted into an adjuvant that is also injected, it is not possible to analyze *the adjuvant is toxic* as an attack. Without this knowledge, this statement could be, for example, purely neutral or irrelevant to the issue.

The conceptual categories used in this short analysis, namely purpose, functions, goals, properties, creation and development, etc., are foundational aspects of the structure of a concept. They allow an accurate identification of statements related to a claim and what facet they exactly attack or support in the issue and how. This is also useful to automatically construct various types of argument synthesis.

The concepts used in attacks and supports related to claim (2) concentrate on facets of humans in society and in the family and evaluates them for women. For example, improving literacy means better education, better jobs and therefore more independence and social recognition, which are typical of the improvement of living conditions. Roughly, the concepts used in statements supporting or attacking claim (2) can be classified into two categories:

– those related to the services provided by society to individuals: education, safety, health, nutrition, human rights, etc. These statements evaluate the quality of these services for women;

– those related to the roles or functions humans can play in society: job and economy development, family development, cultural and social involvement, etc. These statements evaluate if and how women play these roles and functions.

Each of these concepts needs to be structured, as above for the notion of vaccine, to allow an accurate analysis of relatedness. The aim is to identify what facet of women's living conditions these statements support or attack and how. The number of concepts involved may be very large, however, our observations tend to indicate that most arguments concentrate on a few prototypical ones, which are the most striking.

4.2.3. *Observation synthesis*

A synthesis of attacks or supports where the need for knowledge is required to establish relatedness is given in Table 4.2. For example, for claim (1), 44 statements out of a total of 50 (88%) require knowledge to be identified as related to the claim. For these 44 statements, 54 different concepts are required to establish that they are related to claim (1).

From the corpus observations, it turns out that the types of knowledge involved in relating an attack or a support to a claim are based on the existence of relations pertaining to lexical semantics between the concepts of the main terms of the claim and the attack or support. These relations typically include:

– *concepts related via paradigmatic relations*: these include in particular the concepts derived from the head terms of the issue that are either parts or more generic or more specific concepts (hyponyms or hyperonyms) of these head terms. For example, the concept of *adjuvant* is part of the concept *vaccine*, and the notion of *side effect* is a part of the generic concept *medicine*. Iteratively, parts of more generic concepts or subparts of parts are also candidates. The notion of part covers various types of parts, from physical to functional ones [CRU 86]. Transitivity is only valid between parts of the same type. [CRU 86] also addresses a number of methodological problems when defining parts, hyponyms or hyperonyms. To a lesser extent, antonyms have been observed for issues (2) and (3).(e.g. *literacy/lack of education*). These allow to develop attacks between a statement and a claim;

– *concepts related via generic functional relations*: these relations mainly include two classes: (1) those related to the functions, uses, purposes and goals of the concepts in the claim, and (2) those related to the development, construction or creation of the entities represented by the concepts in the claim. The concepts involved in these relations are relatively straightforward for claims that are concrete, such as vaccination, but they are much more complex to specify for more abstract claims, such as claim (2);

– *concepts related via a combination of paradigmatic and functional relations*: the relation between a claim and an attack or a support can be, for example, the purpose of one of the parts of the main concept of the claim. For example, the notion of *industrial independence* associated with claim (3) involves in a more generic concept (a plant, an industrial sector) the functional relation of goal (independence with respect to other countries).

Claim number	Need for knowledge No. of cases (rate)	Total number of concepts involved (rough estimate)
(1)	44 (88%)	54
(2)	21 (77%)	24
(3)	18 (58%)	19
(4)	17 (77%)	27
Total	100 (77%)	124

Table 4.2. *Evidence for knowledge*

The paradigmatic and specific functional relations presented above cover a large majority of the relations between issues and their related arguments, estimated to about 80% of the total. There are obviously other types of relations, which are more difficult to characterize (e.g. *vaccination prevents bioterrorism*), but of much interest for argument mining.

The figures in Table 4.2 show that for about 77% of the statements identified as either attacks or supports, some form of knowledge is involved to establish an argumentative relation with a claim. An important result is that the number of concepts involved is not very large: 124 concepts for 100 statements over four domains. Even if the notion of concept remains vague, these results are, nevertheless, interesting to develop large argument mining systems.

The conceptual organization described in the above analysis tends to suggest that the type of conceptual categorization offered by the Qualia structure, in particular in its last development in Generative Lexicon (GL) [PUS 86], with some extensions to the formalism, is an adequate representation framework to deal with knowledge-based argument mining.

The main other approaches in lexical semantics such as FrameNet or VerbNet mainly concentrate on predicate argument structure for verbs and their adjuncts: they characterize the roles that these elements (NPs, PPs and S) play in the meaning of the verb and the proposition. According to our observations, these are not central features for knowledge-based argument mining, although they may be useful to develop lexical resources (synonyms, antonyms) and argument mining templates as shown in [SAI 16a].

The GL is a model that organizes concept descriptions via structures called roles. Roles describe the purposes and goals of an object or an action, its origin and its uses. These are the main features that are supported or attacked in arguments. These, to the best of our knowledge, are specific features of the GL Qualia structure, in particular the telic and agentive roles. The main limitation is however that the GL has very few resources available. The notions used in the GL Qualia structure are not new: the roles postulated in the Qualia structure are derived from the Aristotelian class of causes, namely constitutive for material, formal for formal, telic for final and agentive for efficient. These roles do not overlap with the notions of grammatical roles or semantic roles. They are much more powerful from the point of view of semantics and knowledge representation.

4.3. Argument synthesis in natural language

A synthesis of the propositions that support or attack a claim is a necessary component of any argument mining system. By synthesis, we mean a structured set of propositions, possibly eliminating redundancies or close-by propositions. In different types of texts and media, it is frequent to mine more than 100 supports or attacks of a given claim, with various strengths and dealing with various facets of the claim. A number of these supports and attacks may largely overlap. It is then difficult and time consuming for users of an argument mining system to read long lists of unstructured propositions where some essential points may not be easily visible due to the amount of data. Looking at how users of argument synthesis proceed, it turns out than even simple forms of synthesis via, for example, clustering techniques could be very useful to make the statements for or against a claim really accessible.

4.3.1. *Features of a synthesis*

So far, very few efforts have been devoted to this aspect of argument mining. Designing an argument synthesis is a delicate task that requires taking into account users' profiles, for example, the type of information that is useful to them, the features which are the most prominent, and the level of granularity they expect. A synthesis must be simple: complex graphs must be avoided since they are rarely legible and understood by users. Carrying out a well-organized synthesis requires the same type of knowledge and conceptual organization as for mining arguments. A synthesis should indeed be closely related to the way arguments are understood.

In natural language generation, the main projects on argumentation generation were developed as early as 2000 by I. Zukerman *et al.* [ZUK 00] and then by A. Fiedler and H. Horacek [FIE 07]. The focus was on the production and the organization of arguments from an abstract semantic representation via some forms of macroplanning, an essential component of natural language generation of texts. A synthesis, and in particular an argument synthesis, is a much simpler operation than the generation of arguments: it consists in grouping already existing propositions related to a claim on the basis of their similarity in order to enhance the reader's understanding and to provide a simple overview. Planning consists in using a hierarchy of concepts so that the most central supports or attacks appear first. A synthesis is therefore more superficial than the generation of arguments.

While there are currently several research efforts to develop argument mining, very little has been done recently to produce a synthesis of the mined arguments that is readable, synthetic enough and relevant for various types of users. This includes identifying the main features for or against a controversial issue, but also eliminating redundancies and various types of fallacies that are less relevant in a synthesis that is aimed at being as neutral as possible. This synthesis may have the form of a short text, possibly including navigation links, or it may take the form of a graphical representation that organizes the reasons or justifications for or against an issue. The major problems are readability, granularity and conceptual adequacy with respect to readers.

In [SAI 16b], it is shown how statements for or against a claim that have been mined can be organized in hierarchically structured clusters, according to the conceptual organization proposed by the GL [PUS 86], so that readers can navigate over and within sets of related statements. This approach turned out not to be synthetic enough, since over 100 reasons can be mined for a given issue, making the perception of the main attacks and supports quite difficult. Nevertheless, this initial approach allows the construction of an argument database with respect to an issue, which is useful to readers who wish to access the exact form of arguments that have been mined. This is illustrated in Figure 4.1, where the relation of each concept to the claim (part of, purpose, etc.) is specified in order to enhance the structure of the description. This figure simply shows a form of synthesis readers would like to have, independently of any knowledge representation consideration.

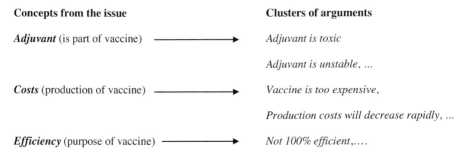

Concepts from the issue   **Clusters of arguments**

Adjuvant (is part of vaccine)   ⟶   *Adjuvant is toxic*

                                         Adjuvant is unstable, ...

Costs (production of vaccine)   ⟶   *Vaccine is too expensive,*

                                         Production costs will decrease rapidly, ...

Efficiency (purpose of vaccine)   ⟶   *Not 100% efficient,....*

Figure 4.1. *Illustration of a synthesis*

It is possible to go one step further. A synthesis can also be viewed as a form of summarization (see section 7.1.2). Various forms of summarization tasks are developed in [MAN 01]. The production of a synthesis that is short and efficient must be carried out at a conceptual level. For example, the concepts present in domain ontologies (as in most opinion analysis systems) or in the GL Qualia structures can be used to abstract over sets of propositions that support or attack an issue at stake. The structure of clusters of propositions is kept and made accessible via links from this synthesis. From that perspective, this work could be viewed as a preliminary step to a summarization procedure. A real summarization task would involve identifying prototypical arguments and themes, and then constructing summaries for each group of related arguments, but this is beyond the state of the art. These concepts can be used as entry points to the cluster system and as a measure of the relevance of a proposition with respect to the issue at stake. A challenging point is that these concepts and their internal organization must correspond as much as possible to the user's perception of the domain to which the issue belongs, otherwise the synthesis may not be so useful.

4.3.2. *Structure of an argumentation synthesis*

Let us now characterize the form of a synthesis, as it can be derived from the examples given in section 4.2.1. Such a synthesis can be organized as follows, starting with the concepts that appear in the claim and then considering those, more remote, which are derived from the concepts of the claim, for example, the properties of the adjuvant are derived concepts, since the adjuvant is a part of a vaccine.

To make the synthesis readable and informative, the total number of occurrences of arguments mined in texts for that concept is given between parentheses, as an indication. The goal is to outline strengths, recurrences and tendencies. This, however, remains informal because occurrence frequencies are very much dependent on how many texts have been processed and how many attacks or supports have been mined. This number is also used as a link that points to the statements that have been mined in their original textual form. For each line, the positive facet is presented first, followed by the negative one when it exists, independently of the occurrence frequency, in order to preserve a certain homogeneity in the reading:

> *Vaccine protection is good (3), bad (5).*
> *Vaccine avoids (5), does not avoid (3) dissemination.*
> *Vaccine is difficult (3) to develop.*
> *Vaccine is expensive (4).*
> *Vaccine is not (1) available.*
> *Ebola is (5) a dangerous disease.*
> *Humans may die (1) from Ebola.*
> *Tests of the vaccine show no (2) high (4) side effects.*
> *Other arguments (4).*

Each line of the synthesis can be produced via a predefined language pattern [SAI 17]. The comprehensive list of supports and attacks is stored in clusters as described above. They are accessible via navigation links, represented in this synthesis by means of underlined numbers.

An alternative synthesis approach would have been to select for each concept a support or an attack that is prototypical, with a link to the other statements related to the same concept. This approach sounds less artificial than the generation of abstract sentences, but (1) it is difficult to characterize what a prototypical statement is and (2) the formulation proposed above is *a priori* shorter, more neutral and more standardized. However, we feel that exploring other forms of synthesis, in close cooperation with users, should be investigated. For example, forms of rhetoric could be incorporated for non-neutral synthesis where, for example, some emphasis must be put on certain points. Introductions to these aspects can be found, among many others, in [PER 77] and in [AMO 10] who develops specific cases related to news editorials.

5

From Argumentation to Argument Mining

Argument mining is still in an early stage of development. It raises much more complex challenges than information retrieval or question answering. Answering *Why*-questions in question answering could be the closest related challenge, if we consider that its main aim is to retrieve justifications to a claim. In contrast with information retrieval and question answering, mining attacks or supports to a claim cannot, in most cases, be based solely on linguistic cues, as shown in Chapter 4, since they are not very frequent or central. When linguistic cues exist, they can be ambiguous and may introduce, for example, causes or factual information, besides attacks or supports. Argument delimitation is also a real challenge.

Argumentation is a very complex phenomenon, and argument mining is just an approximation or a simplification of some aspects of argumentation analysis in order to extract prototypical arguments or parts of them with a reasonably good accuracy. Argument mining also depends on the goal that is pursued, for example, detecting fallacies, finding arguments, detecting argumentation strategies, finding claims, finding support or attack for a given stance, among others.

5.1. Some facets of argument mining

Due to these complexities, most of the projects aiming at automatically detecting arguments in text focus on argument annotations in various manners. Reliable, stable annotation from experts is required to build automatic systems. The goal of working on the annotation of argumentative texts is first to have a better understanding of how arguments are produced and how they can be systematized (see Chapter 6). Then, from annotations, learning methods can be applied that should allow the implementation of efficient argument recognition processes (see Chapters 7 and 8). This includes the recognition of claims, on the one hand, and attacks or justifications, on the other hand.

Annotating arguments is a very difficult task, probably due to the inherent complexity of the processes involved and to the high interpretative subjectivity of the task. Even with extensive annotation guidelines and training, low interannotator agreement levels are often observed in annotation efforts. Disagreement is found in virtually all aspects of annotation. Chapter 6 presents a diversity of views on the different aspects and how they are addressed to enhance the reliability of annotation.

As we will see in Chapter 7, argument mining is explored in various domains and genres, where difficulties and challenges may be very different. Different genres may employ very different language features, for example in news editorials, online forums or political debates. Argument mining is of much importance in – oral or online – debates [BUD 14b, SWA 15], and in more specific forms such as litigation and deliberations. Oral debates are usually transcribed as plain text before arguments are mined. Features related to orality such as prosody and intonation, which are useful to determine argument strength, are lost in this process. Punctuation, silences and other surface forms are also frequently lost (see also Chapter 9).

The first challenge that is frequently dealt with is, in a single text identified as argumentative (e.g. news editorial), to mine for claims, with probably a main claim and secondary claims. Argumentative texts include the expression of juridical decisions, political debates or scientific articles (e.g. [MOC 09, NGU 15, GRE 17]). A useful and comprehensive survey is provided in [PEL 13].

Both argumentative texts and debates may contain several unrelated claims and subclaims. For example, in a political or in a juridical debate, several points of equal importance, and possibly related, may be debated. A debate is usually less organized than an argumentative text, with a large number of non-adjacent relations between claims and their related supports or attacks. Moreover, the fact that there may be more than one party in the discussion makes it more complex to analyze and mine.

Once claims are identified, another challenge is to identify supports and attacks and the various relations between arguments. A more complex version of this task is, given a claim, to find supports or attacks to that claim through texts from various sources. This task shares some aspects of question answering: a claim can be viewed as a question and supports or attacks as answers. This latter task raises difficult linguistic and reasoning problems, which have been presented in Chapter 4. In the remainder of this book, in order to limit complexity, only topics related to argument mining in single argumentative texts and in debates, as described above, are developed.

Argument annotation often requires taking into account pragmatic and implicit aspects. For example, annotators have to deal with presuppositions left implicit by speakers or authors. They have to reconstruct them on the basis of their own knowledge and value system, or the value systems they think authors have. They also have to take into account forms of stress, emphasis and irony that are frequent in debates (see also section 6.1.9). Another difficulty is the identification of the argument schemes that have been used [MUS 16]: these are crucial to evaluate the strength of a support or an attack and, on a larger scale, to evaluate the validity of arguments.

Besides the identification of the features of claims and supports or attacks, annotation tasks reveal the practices and the contrasts between the various areas and genres where argumentation is important if not the rule, for example, deliberations (e.g. [WAL 12]), juridical debates, opinion analysis (e.g. [VIL 12]) and mediation. Annotated corpora allow for an accurate analysis and cognitive modeling of the types of reasoning that are prevalent in each genre (see section 6.5).

5.2. Designing annotation guidelines: some methodological elements

Similarly to investigations on a number of natural language aspects, argument structure analysis is essentially based on annotation efforts, which are frequently improved by the use of resources such as terminologies and lexical semantics data as well as syntactic and discourse parsers. Argument mining is a process that is partial: usually only some aspects of argumentation are investigated and annotated. Argument annotation is a difficult task that requires very well-trained annotators who must, besides linguistic competence, have a relatively good understanding of the domain that is covered by the annotation task, such as US politics, European history, or business and international finance. Indeed, without at least a moderate understanding of the domain in which arguments are annotated, annotators find it difficult to make correct decisions on, for example, the fact that a statement is a justification of a claim or on the orientation of a statement (support or attack).

The annotation of a phenomenon that has not yet been the subject of annotation, such as arguments, and their related claims, supports and attacks, is generally done in several steps. First, there is an exploration phase where the parameters that could be annotated are investigated. Accuracy, stability, reproducibility, appropriate granularity level, clear scope and minimal ambiguity level are useful properties that must be checked. Then the importance of each parameter is questioned, together with the feasibility of its implementation in an annotation, its complexity as well as the linguistic resources and analytical capabilities from existing methods, which can be used. A crucial question is then how deep to annotate arguments, where there is a clear trade-off between model complexity and annotation reliability and overall quality.

Once the preliminary investigation has been undertaken, a first version of annotation guidelines is produced, which is often very descriptive of what to do and what to avoid. These guidelines are used to train annotators, who can test them at the same time. Via annotator return of experience, guidelines can be gradually improved, until they reach a certain stability and level of abstraction. Reaching such a maturity level may require several years for complex tasks such as annotating debates. It is therefore crucial to proceed gradually and to develop simple indicative evaluations at each step. Annotation guidelines can become unusable or useless if they are not elaborated with great care, with a clear method and frequent evaluation steps. Several annotation schemes are presented in the chapters that follow. The reader can note that these are not necessarily compatible: they develop various features of argument mining, with different perspectives, that depend, for example, on the type of task that is being realized.

For example, one method is to gradually identify and annotate claims, attacks and supports considered in isolation. Then, in a second step, claims, on the one hand, and attacks or supports, on the other hand, could be bound. It is important at this level to assume that arguments are relatively rational, with satisfactory regularity of expression, no irony and no complex references. Then, the next task is to analyze the lexical data in the material that has been annotated in terms of lexical data, as presented in Chapter 4, and structure these various lexical forms for the purpose of making a synthesis. In Chapter 8, an implementation example is given that shows how lexical data can be structured and the type of lexical and semantic data that are needed. For example, it is important to decide on their real use and possible generalizations to other terms not found in the texts considered. Furthermore, it is useful to extend them with synonyms: the class of verbs expressing agreement, doubt and any other propositional attitude can then be enriched. The following task is to define semantic features that are appropriate in terms of content and granularity. Then the goal is to stabilize these features and define guidelines with a certain abstraction level that could be re-used in a number of related situations.

Argument mining is essentially achieved from surface linguistic and typographic considerations. It may be simpler to consider specific types of arguments or specific types of applications and domains (e.g. news, scientific articles). The development of learning methods to characterize argument forms on these restricted areas produces more accurate systems. The considerations and concerns presented in this section are developed in detail in Chapters 6 and 7.

5.3. What results can be expected from an argument mining system?

The simplest elements that can be expected from an argument mining system are, from the simplest to the most complex ones:

– the identification of claims, also called viewpoints or stances, when these are not given *a priori* (contrary to a question–answering system);

– the identification of the statements related to these claims;

– the analysis of whether these statements can act as justifications to form arguments, and their orientation (attack or support); this includes the delimitation of the text span that represents the statement;

– the identification of the strength inherent to each attack and support;

– the identification of duplicates or very similar statements, for example, to eliminate redundancies in a synthesis or to analyze strength;

– the identification of the argument scheme that has been used for each claim–support or claim–attack pair, and the identification of those which are the most frequent in a certain type of argumentative text;

– the identification of fallacies and other forms of invalid arguments; the linguistic and rhetorical means used for that purpose may be of interest for sociological analysis;

– for a given claim, the construction of a synthesis that helps readers to have an overall understanding of the pros and cons related to that claim, with their strength and occurrence frequencies. Argumentation graphs may be useful to represent small sets of supports or attacks;

– for complex texts, an overview of the structure of claims and secondary claims, and in a debate the position of each participant;

– for situations that last for a long period of time, the temporal evolution of arguments possibly giving new information.

The evaluation of argument mining systems is in an early development stage. At the moment, evaluation by components is carried out based on manually annotated test corpora. However, due to low interannotator agreement levels, evaluation remains purely indicative and subject to discussions. This is discussed in Chapter 6.

5.4. Architecture of an argument mining system

The architecture of an argument mining system can be described through its components. Different strategies may be applied: either the different components are developed in a kind of pipeline architecture (one after the other), where components are recognized after the others, or in a more integrated way so that features of a subsequent level can be used to resolve the ambiguities found at a previous level.

The classical overall architecture of a modular, pipeline-based argument mining system can be summarized as follows. First, a module delimits argument components within an argumentative text. Then, the relations between these argument components are determined, probably distinguishing submodules like classifying argument components into different types (claim, premise) and establishing relations between them (attack, support) or filling slots in a template. This is discussed in Chapter 7.

In the last years, end-to-end architectures have also been proposed, applying neural approaches (see, for instance, [POT 17] or [EGE 17]). These architectures deal with all the tasks separated by modular architectures at the same time, with complex convolutional neural networks that learn all tasks jointly. They obtain state-of-the-art results with arguably less effort in crafting features for machine learning methods.

5.5. The next chapters

In the rest of the book, we will be presenting how different aspects of argumentation are addressed with the goal of mining them automatically. We will mainly be focusing on how annotation efforts deal with the complexity of argumentation and how they try to delimit concepts and to systematize their identification in texts, in order to obtain reliable, reproducible annotations. In the following chapter, we outline the annotation process and how the different aspects of annotation are interrelated. We also describe some tools and metrics that allow the assessment of reproducibility. In Chapter 7, we give an overview of a few automatic argument mining systems.

Annotation Frameworks and Principles of Argument Analysis

Research in linguistics mostly relies on empirical analyses to characterize or understand a discourse feature. Corpus analyses are particularly useful because they provide detailed and thorough information about peculiar discourse characteristics.

In computational linguistics, manual annotations of naturally occurring examples have been used as a source of training material. This task consists in annotators manually assigning an interpretation to texts.

Argumentation theorists carry out annotations of texts to detect, identify and evaluate arguments. This analytical task is necessary to understand and characterize facets of human reasoning. Manually annotating argumentative texts, indeed, allows the detection of argumentative components which may not be anticipated. It is also necessary to manually perform annotations prior to building systems that can automatically replicate them afterwards. Moreover, argument analyses can be used to provide examples and counterexamples of argument features in order to feed a program that will automatically detect them or to develop rules and grammars. In other words, annotated data are used as training sets to test and develop argument mining systems.

In this chapter, we describe some annotation frameworks (or models) that have been used to analyze arguments, with an emphasis on the different argument elements that can (or must) be identified and analyzed. We also emphasize the need for clearly defined guidelines to provide accurate analyses. Some annotation tools allowing the analysis of argument are also presented.

6.1. Principles of argument analysis

A set of theoretical frameworks has been developed for the description, analysis or evaluation of arguments. These theories are applied to annotate natural language argumentation. They do not all aim at examining the same characteristics of argumentation; however, most of them focus on the main argument elements, including those identified by Toulmin (see Chapter 2.2.1). Indeed, understanding arguments, and by extension automatically detecting argumentation, requires understanding different elements of discourse. Such elements are varied and bear their own complexity, as much for human annotators as for computational systems. We present here several such elements and show how they can help us understand argumentation.

Analyzing arguments in naturally occurring texts consists in two main tasks: first, raw texts must be segmented (usually to distinguish argumentative units from non-argumentative ones), then argumentative components must be assigned a type (usually predefined in the theoretical framework at stake). Thus, some approaches limit themselves to the identification of claims and possibly premises, while other theories classify components in finer-grained and specific classes. We intend in the following sections to give an account of the various classes and components that can be annotated with respect to argumentation.

Note that the final application of an argument mining system is decisive of the annotation process: the annotated components will be different based on what the system is trying to achieve. For instance, if the system aims at reconstructing the argument structure of a text, the annotation process will take into account argumentative elements that may not need to be analyzed if the system was developed to simply detect main claims.

6.1.1. *Argumentative discourse units*

When annotating a text to analyze arguments, it is necessary to first determine the text parts that bear an argumentative function. In the literature, these are called Argumentative Discourse Units (ADUs). As a matter of fact, in a text, not all sentences bear an argumentative function. See, for instance, the following sentence taken from a radio debate:

> *Our panel, Claire Fox from the Institute of Ideas, the former Conservative Cabinet Minister Michael Portillo, the Catholic writer Clifford Longley and the science historian Kenan Malik.*[1]

---

1 This example is extracted from a BBC radio program *The Moral Maze*, a moderated debate in which panelists and witnesses are invited to discuss social, political and economical current issues.

In this example, the speaker (i.e. the moderator) introduces the panelists who will participate in the debate. Defining whether this move has an argumentative function or not is a tricky task. Intuitively, and without any context, this move does not seem to have an argumentative function since it does not help the speaker build an argument and it is not attacked. Although it would seem irrelevant and unreasonable to attack this move (i.e. to provide counterarguments), an opponent could, theoretically, disagree with the sentence, or parts of it. For instance, s/he could disagree that Kenan Malik is a science historian.

Nevertheless, determining whether a move plays a role in the argument cannot rely on intuition. Note that a proposition can be considered as a simple *fact* when it has no support or attack and if it does not contain an evaluative element. For instance, "Nice is a city in southern France" is not a claim, while "Nice is a sunny city" is a claim: *sunny* is a scalable evaluative element (see section 3.1) and, although no supporting claim is provided, one can imagine that the utterer may provide a premise or else a listener may attack it. Manually segmenting a text into ADUs may represent the first and most complex task of argument analysis. Let us now have a look at another example:

> *Vaccines have allowed reducing the number of deaths. Not just in Africa but worldwide.*

This example is composed of two sentences. While it might seem logical to segment it into two parts ("vaccines have allowed reducing the number of deaths" and "not just in Africa but worldwide"), actually, the ADU is the entire example since it has one single propositional content "Vaccines have allowed reducing the number of deaths not just in Africa but worldwide": both sentences are *glued* together. Therefore, one cannot necessarily rely on punctuation to segment a text into ADUs. Rather, it is common to consider that an argumentative segment must contain one single proposition whether it is composed of one sentence (in a grammatical sense) or more.

The problem of properly segmenting also arises when a proposition is interrupted by another proposition (particularly common in dialogical contexts, but not exclusively). Let us take the following example:

> *Speaker 1: Vaccines are essential...*
> *Speaker 2: Sure.*
> *Speaker 1: ... to prevent diseases.*

In this example, Speaker 2 interrupts Speaker 1. However, the first ADU must contain Speaker 1's both utterances: "vaccines are essential to prevent diseases"; then, the second ADU is "sure".

Segmenting an argumentative text therefore is challenging: first, one has to delimit units, then one must determine whether each unit is argumentative or not.

Some units, taken in isolation may not be (or seem) argumentative, but their argumentative character depends on other units. Note that "argumentative" does not equal "subjective" or "opinionated", since some argument components are clearly factual. H. Wachsmuth *et al.* [WAC 17] state that "a comment should be seen as argumentative if you think that it explicitly or implicitly conveys the stance of the comment's author on some possibly controversial issue." Different methods (guidelines) exist to segment a text, depending on the analytical framework at stake; some examples are given in section 6.3.

6.1.2. *Conclusions and premises*

Also called *main claims*, conclusions are claims that must be defended (since this is where the principal controversy may lie). A way to defend a main claim is by providing supporting claims called *premises*. Broadly speaking, a claim originates two standpoints: the claim itself and its negation. Let us take the following example:

> *Vaccination campaigns are essential. They prevent the propagation of diseases.*

The main claim here is the ADU "vaccination campaigns are essential" (one can negate this statement); it is supported by one premise (a second ADU) "they [vaccination campaigns] prevent the propagation of diseases". A simple XML annotation of this argument would be:

```
<argument>
<conclusion> Vaccination campaigns are essential. </conclusion>
<premise> They prevent the propagation of diseases. </premise>
</argument>.
```

During the annotation process, guidelines and hints can be provided to ease the detection of main claims; these may include the consideration of:

– discourse connectives like "in conclusion", "therefore";

– the position in the document, mostly in the introduction or the conclusion;

– the presence of verbs or nouns indicating stance or belief as "claim", "believe", etc.

Although these indicators may help the annotators, their utility is limited, in particular because they are not always frequent in texts; but in some domains or genres – like academic writing – the usage of discourse connectives is more frequent, more systematic and less ambiguous than in open-domain texts (see sections 3.1 and 3.2).

6.1.3. *Warrants and backings*

A *warrant* is a justification rule (a generally accepted truth, applying to most circumstances); it justifies the logical inference from the premise to the claim. A *backing* supports a warrant (it is a generalization rule such as a physical law); it is a set of information that assures the warrant trustworthiness. These elements are often implicit but can be reconstructed; as Toulmin says "data are appealed to explicitly, warrants implicitly" [TOU 03, p 92]. In the following example,

> *It's freezing this morning: flowers will suffer.*

the first ADU is "it's freezing this morning" (a premise) and the second ADU (the main claim) is "flowers will suffer". A possible warrant would be "flowers do not like freezing weather" and a possible backing would be a law of botany explaining why flowers do not like frost (see also section 2.2.1). If this reconstruction is chosen, a possible simple annotation would be:

```
<argument>
<premise> It's freezing this morning: </premise>
<warrant> flowers do not like freezing weather </warrant>
<backing> a law of botany explains that flowers do not like frost </backing>
<conclusion> flowers will suffer. </conclusion>
</argument>.
```

6.1.4. *Qualifiers*

A *qualifier* indicates the strength of the inferential link between a premise and a conclusion. In other words, it indicates the confidence of an utterer in her conclusion. In the following example (annotated below), the qualifier is the word "surely". As an illustration, the qualifier has an attribute "strength" that represents its impact:

> *It's freezing this morning: flowers will surely suffer.*

```
<argument>
<premise> It's freezing this morning: </premise>
<conclusion> flowers will <qualifier strength="high"> surely </qualifier> suffer.
</conclusion>
</argument>.
```

Qualifiers are not always easily identified: in "Vaccines prevent most diseases", the strength of the claim is lowered by the word *most*. Moreover, as many other argument components such as warrants and backings, qualifiers are not always explicit; hence, in [HAB 17], in spite of their use of Toulmin's model in the annotation process, the authors decided not to analyze qualifiers because they found out that arguers rarely indicate the "degree of congency" (i.e. the probability/strength of their claims).

6.1.5. *Argument schemes*

Argument schemes are patterns of reasoning. A detailed (yet non-exhaustive) list of such patterns is provided by Walton *et al.* [WAL 08]. Argument schemes, indeed, are various ([WAL 08] provides a set of 60 argument schemes) and sometimes hard to distinguish (see sections 2.5 and 3.3, or [WAL 15b] for a classification). Argument schemes are non-textual elements, therefore they are implicit argument elements that have to be identified and reconstructed. As we will see later on, this is a challenge that scholars have tackled more or less successfully (see, for instance, [LAW 16]). Let us take the following example that may be analyzed as an *argument from analogy* (see section 2.5.3):

> *It has been shown that vaccinating against malaria can be useless in some cases; similarly the vaccine against Ebola is not recommended.*

<argument ="argument from analogy">
<premise> It has been shown that vaccinating against malaria can be useless in some cases; </premise>
<conclusion> similarly, the vaccine against Ebola is not recommended. </conclusion>
</argument>.

6.1.6. *Attack relations: rebuttals, refutations, undercutters*

Arguments suppose a (sometimes implicit) opposition: all argument components can be *attacked* by providing new claims. Therefore, premises of an argument can be attacked as well as its conclusion. Note that, if we consider the dialectical nature of argumentation, proponents as well as opponents can provide supports for claims. As a result, when an opponent puts forward a claim attacking a proponent's argument, s/he can provide support (premises) for this attacking claim, which creates a *counterargument* or *rebuttal*. In monological contexts, one can provide counterarguments for several reasons, including to anticipate an attack; a *refutation* is when this attack is then itself attacked. Let us take the following example (taken from the AIFdb Corpus *Moral Maze British Empire*[2]).

> *You say that Britain is non-inclusive, but I mean, relative to many other countries surely it's an exemplar of inclusivity.*

In this example, the speaker attacks what his opponent said previously in the dialogue, namely that *Britain is non-inclusive*: according to him, Britain *is an exemplar of inclusivity*.

---

2 http://corpora.aifdb.org/britishempire.

In Toulmin's model, *rebuttals* are conditions that may undermine an inference: they attack a qualifier. In other words, rebuttals present a situation in which a claim might be defeated. A possible rebuttal for the example presented in section 6.1.4 above would be "unless the flowers are protected". Rebuttals can be explicitly stated in an argument in order to show exceptions to the defended claim or to anticipate an attack.

<argument>
<premise> It's freezing this morning: </premise>
<conclusion> flowers will <qualifier strength="high"> surely </qualifier> suffer.
</conclusion>
<rebuttal> unless the flowers are protected </rebuttal>
</argument>.

I. Habernal [HAB 14, p 27] proposes the following definition to detect rebuttals and refutations:

> *Rebuttal* attacks the main claim by presenting an opponent's view. In most cases, the rebuttal is again attacked by the author using *refutation*. Refutation thus supports the author's stance expressed by the claim. So it can be confused with grounds, as both provide reasons for the claim. Refutation thus only takes place if it is meant as a reaction to the rebuttal. It follows the discussed matter and contradicts it. Such a discourse can be mainly expressed as: [rebuttal: On the other hand, some people say that my Claim is wrong.] [refutation: But this is not true, because of that and that.]

A way of attacking the strength of arguments is to provide a claim attacking the validity of an inference; in the literature such claims are called *undercutters* (for instance, [PEL 13]). Undercutters allow showing that the inferential link does not hold. For instance, J.L. Pollock [POL 95] considers the example of a red object: two premises to assert that "the object is red" are "the object looks red" and "things that look red are normally red"; a way of attacking this argument would be to claim that "the object is illuminated by a red light": this claim attacks the link between "the object looks red and things that look red are normally red" (premises) and "this object is red" (conclusion).

Undercutters are somewhat difficult to represent in a language such as XML, which is basically linear or flat. We suggest below, but there are other possibilities, to include the undercutter as an attribute of the tag 'argument', which qualifies the nature of the relation between the premise and the conclusion and the potential difficulties associated with this relation:

<argument undercutter="the object is illuminated by a red light">
<conclusion> The object is red </conclusion>
<premise1> the object looks red </premise1>

<premise2> things that look red are normally red </premise2>
</argument>.

Attack relations in argumentation are therefore various and sometimes hard to distinguish (as shown in Habernal's quote above). Moreover, they may not appear at all but one might want to consider them in an argument analysis.

6.1.7. *Illocutionary forces, speech acts*

Some works in argumentation are interested in determining the arguer's intentions. According to Speech Act Theory (SAT), utterances (spoken or written) are thought to be propositional contents to which a force (the illocutionary force) is attached [SEA 69]. This force represents the intention (or position) of the utterer with regard to the propositional content. S/he can claim, question, challenge, reject, etc. SAT, therefore, offers a valuable framework in which utterances can be described and analyzed according to their force.

J.R. Searle and D. Vanderveken [SEA 85] classify illocutionary forces in five categories: assertives, commissives, directives, declaratives and expressives. These categories allow a first general distinction between locutors' communicative intentions. Knowing what the speakers' intentions are is crucial for understanding a particular discourse: if a speaker/writer claims something (assertive verb), this means that he (normally) believes what he says; if he uses an expressive verb (e.g. to apologize), he shows his attitude, rather than opinion, toward the propositional content. An approach that makes extensive use of SAT is pragma-dialectics [EEM 03]. In this theory, the analysis of discourse relies on a normative framework in which the speakers' communicative intentions must always be analyzed.

A drawback of SAT is that it does not capture the interaction between utterances. The framework does not tell us anything about the discourse resulting from exchanges of utterances, which is crucial to understand dialogues. Moreover, despite the great value of SAT as a theoretical framework for studying language use, it is inadequate for the description of argumentation [EEM 82]. Inference Anchoring Theory (IAT) [BUD 11], an analytical framework for dialogical argumentation, is based on SAT: it allows the representation of the structure of argumentative dialogues by eliciting the illocutionary forces of locutions (e.g. [BUD 14c]). This framework tackles what SAT fails at capturing: the relationship between sequences of speech acts. With the representation of the argumentative structure as a final goal, IAT makes it possible to show how arguments are constructed through dialogical exchanges (see section 6.2.3 for more details). Let us take the following dialogue and its annotation taken from [BUD 14c][3]:

---

3 A complete argument map is available at http://corpora.aifdb.org/mm2012; it shows that the relationship between the first and second ADUs is one of counterargument (or disagreement),

> *Lawrence James: It was a ghastly aberration.*
> *Clifford Longley: Or was it in fact typical? Was it the product of a*
> *policy that was unsustainable that could only be pursued by increasing*
> *repression?*

<utterance speaker = "lj" illoc = "standard_assertion">
<textunit nb = "215"> it was a ghastly aberration </textunit> </utterance>.
<utterance speaker = "cl" illoc = "RQ">
<textunit nb = "216"> or was it in fact typical ? </textunit> </utterance> .
<utterance speaker = "cl" illoc = "RQ-AQ">
<textunit nb = "217"> was it the product of a policy that was unsustainable that could
only be pursued by increasing repression? </textunit> </utterance>.

6.1.8. *Argument relations*

Once all the argumentative components have been identified and classified according to their type (i.e. when each unit is given a label corresponding to its type, e.g. main claim, premise, rebuttal, conflict, argument scheme), it can be of interest to show the relationship between them. For instance, when two premises are identified, one can wonder whether they work independently (convergent arguments) or whether they function together to support the conclusion (linked arguments). Equally, one can wonder whether an attack points to a premise, a conclusion or an inferential link for instance.

Identifying the component to which another component is linked may be a very difficult task, because there may be long-distance relations between arguments, possibly spanning paragraphs, in particular for texts with a complex argumentative structure, like scientific papers or judgments. Finding relations between components is challenging, usually returning low interannotator agreement (IAA) results and poor performance in automated systems (see sections 6.3 and 7.3).

The primary inventory of relations is the *attack/support* distinction. These two relations capture the most basic role of components in an argument, that is, if the component is providing more strength (support) or undermining the strength (attack) of a given claim.

Representation of arguments as trees (as in Toulmin's model) misses the ability to show multiple relations of argumentation. The presentation of argumentation relations as graphs is therefore more convenient as attack relations as well as supports and interconnections between argument components can also be represented. In such graphical representations, claims are usually represented as nodes and the relations between nodes take the form of directed arrows.

---

while the second and third ADUs form an argument. More details on these annotations are given in section 6.2.3.

Figure 6.1, taken from [OKA 08, p. 4], shows an argument map realized with the Rationale argument analysis tool (see section 6.4.5 for more details); each node contains one claim, the top one being the main claim (conclusion) linked to the others via arrows: green ones represent supports and red ones attacks.

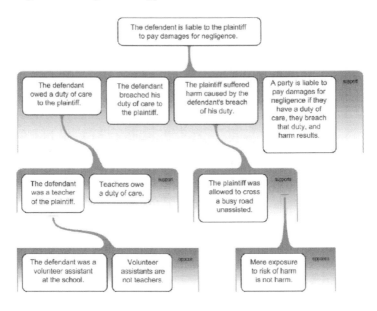

Figure 6.1. *An argument map with Rationale. For a color version of this figure, see www.iste.co.uk/janier/argument.zip*

Although most models follow similar rules for the graphical representation of argumentation analyses, some differences may appear as their purposes are not always akin. As an example, in Peldszus and Stede's [PEL 13] model, claims uttered by a proponent appear in box nodes and attacks appear in circle nodes. Figure 6.2, taken from [PEL 13, p. 19], is the graphical argument structure of the manual analysis of the following text:

> *[The building is full of asbestos,]₁ [so we should tear it down.]₂ [In principle it is possible to clean it up,]₃ [but according to the mayor that would be forbiddingly expensive.]₄*

In the manual analysis, the text has been segmented and four segments have been identified. The relationships between the segments are represented in Figure 6.2, where (1) the segments are represented by their corresponding numbers in the manual annotation above, (2) directed arrows show support links and (3) round-headed arrows show attacks.

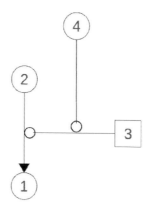

Figure 6.2. *An argument diagram*

Figure 6.3, taken from [BUD 16, p. 93], presents another type of argument graph. This graphical representation of the dialogue below relies on the IAT model (see sections 6.1.7 and 6.2).

> *Bob: p is the case.*
> *Wilma: Why p?*
> *Bob: q.*

IAT being mostly used in dialogical contexts, speakers' locutions are represented (on the right-hand side of the analysis) because the argumentative structure is derived from the analysis of dialogue dynamics. This type of analysis allows to show dialogical dynamics and their attached argumentative structures and explicit illocutionary connections. Here, the second speaker *challenged* the first speaker's utterance that triggers argumentation (see the support relation, instantiated by the *rule application* node). As we will see later, other argument components can be annotated with IAT, such as additional illocutionary connections or attack relations among others.

Figures 6.1–6.3 show that annotating arguments can take various forms according to what the model is used for but they follow the same principles: eliciting argument relations in order to grasp the subtleties of reasoning in different contexts.

6.1.9. *Implicit argument components and tailored annotation frameworks*

We have just seen that many argumentative components (such as warrants, backings or illocutionary forces) are often left implicit. According to Habernal and

Gurevych [HAB 17], even the main components of argumentation can be implicit: in their study of web discourse, the unrestricted environment (and their method) required the main claim (actually the stance toward a topic) to be inferred by annotators.

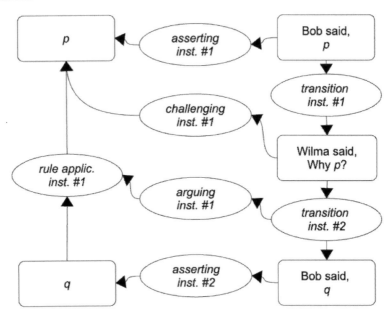

Figure 6.3. *An IAT argument map*

Some research is interested in identifying (and expliciting) implicit argument components. As a matter of fact, some works focus on evaluating argumentation rather than just analyzing it: some underlying characteristics of arguments must therefore be identified.

In order to enable the detection and analysis of argumentation – including implicit elements – and to address specific domains, genres or a specific application, many researchers have designed their own *annotation frameworks*. As a result, and as we have just seen in the different graphical representations, the analysis of some components mentioned in the sections above may be of no interest in a certain annotation effort, whereas, for others, more fine-grained annotation schemes may be required (i.e. more labels). As an example, S. Teufel *et al.* [TEU 99b] annotate elements such as *background* (general scientific background), *other* (neutral descriptions of other people's work) or *own* (neutral description of the author's new work) in scientific articles; similarly, K. Al-Khatib *et al.* [ALK 16] propose classes such as *common ground* (an accepted truth) or *assumption* (a general observation, possibly false) in newspapers editorials.

6.2. Examples of argument analysis frameworks

In this section, we propose a brief overview of some analytical frameworks in order to show the diversity of argument models.

6.2.1. *Rhetorical Structure Theory*

Rhetorical Structure Theory (RST) is a descriptive theory that aims at eliciting rhetorical relations in written texts [MAN 88]. RST allows revealing the structure of natural language texts by showing the different relations between text portions. A wide range of such relations has been identified (e.g. justification, elaboration and restatement), which allow a comprehensive analysis of the hierarchical structure of texts. In RST, the writer's intention, i.e. what he intends to rhetorically achieve in his discourse, must be taken into account.

This model was not primarily developed for argumentation but for rhetorical relations. Despite the drawbacks that this represents, some works (such as [PEL 13]) have shown that arguments can, nevertheless, be analyzed since the writer/speaker's intentions and changes in the reader/listener's attitude/beliefs are at stake. For instance, RST's scheme allows to elicit *justification, evidence, motivation, antithesis* or *concession* relations. RST analyses take the form of tree-like structures where arrows connect *satellites* to a *nucleus*. Two major limitations of the model is that (1) only adjacent segments can be analyzed and (2) no parts of the text must be left non-analyzed. M. Azar [AZA 99] uses RST as an annotation tool rather than a theoretical frameworks, shifting RST's original purpose.

Although RST central idea of functional relations to describe discourse structure subsumes taking into account the writers' rhetorical aims, the model is not interested in speech acts (or illocutionary forces), and misses the opportunity to describe their intentions. RST, primarily designed for written texts, has been expanded to be applied to dialogues. The model indeed fails to capture the structure of dialogues. As a response to this weakness, A. Stent [STE 00] has modified some RST guidelines and added annotation schemes that allow showing the hierarchical rhetorical structure between argumentative acts in task-oriented dialogues.

Figure 6.4 shows an RST analysis of the text below (both taken from [CAR 03, p. 91]). The different segments are represented by their corresponding numbers in the manual analysis and relations between components are elicited with arrows (from *nucleus* to *satellite*) and identified by labels (*example, consequence*, etc.).

[Still, analysts don't expect the buy-back to significantly affect per-share earnings in the short term.][16] [The impact won't be that great,][17][said Graeme Lidgerwood of First Boston Corp.][18] [This is in part because of the effect][19] [of having to average the number of shares outstanding,][20] [she said.][21] [In addition,][22] [Mrs. Lidgerwood said,][23] [Norfolk is likely to draw down its cash initially][24] [to finance the purchases][25] [and thus forfeit some interest income.][26]

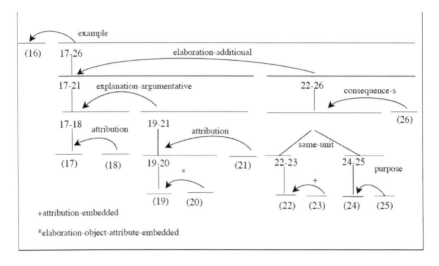

Figure 6.4. *An RST analysis*

6.2.2. *Toulmin's model*

Many research works have relied on Toulmin's vision of what an argument is, especially argument visualization frameworks. This model is therefore the cornerstone of many argumentation theories (e.g. [FRE 11, WAL 96]). Despite its high value as a theoretical model, Toulmin's model often fails at accurately capturing argumentation (e.g. as argued in [NEW 91, HIT 06]). As a result, many researchers have modified the model to satisfy their needs. For instance, I. Habernal and I. Gurevych [HAB 17] propose a *modified Toulmin model* to annotate texts taken from the web. Indeed, the authors do not annotate qualifiers and warrants but add a category *refutation* to their tailored scheme. As a result, their analysis framework contains five elements: claim, grounds, backing, rebuttal and refutation. Figure 6.5 is an example of their manual analysis, and Figure 6.6 shows the graphical representation.

Doc#4733 (forumpost, public-private-schools) [*claim:* The public schooling system is not as bad as some may think.] [*rebuttal:* Some mentioned that those who are educated in the public schools are less educated,] [*refutation:* well I actually think it would be in the reverse.] [*premise:* Student who study in the private sector actually pay a fair amount of fees to do so and I believe that the students actually get let off for a lot more than anyone would in a public school. And its all because of the money.¶ In a private school, a student being expelled or suspended is not just one student out the door, its the rest of that students schooling life fees gone. Whereas in a public school, its just the student gone.]¶ [*backing:* I have always gone to public schools and when I finished I got into University. I do not feel disadvantaged at all.]

Figure 6.5. *A manual analysis, taken from [HAB 17, p. 144]*

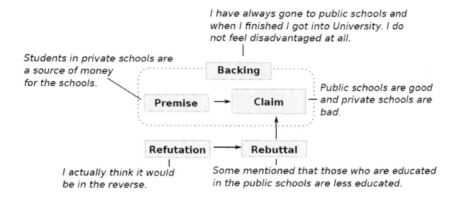

Figure 6.6. *A graphical representation following Toulmin's model, taken from [HAB 17, p. 144]*

6.2.3. *Inference Anchoring Theory*

We have seen in sections 6.1.7 and 6.1.8 that Inference Anchoring Theory (IAT) [BUD 11] is an analytical framework for dialogues. It allows to represent the structure of argumentative dialogues by eliciting the illocutionary forces of locutions (e.g. [BUD 14c]). The expression "argumentative structure" cannot be separated from IAT: it has to be understood as "the shape of the discussion", i.e. how the discussants' moves in a dialogue work together to create argumentation. Grounded in SAT (see section 6.1.7), this framework tackles what SAT fails at capturing: the relationship between sequences of speech acts. With the representation of the argumentative structure as a final goal, IAT makes it possible to show how arguments are constructed through dialogical exchanges. Designed to allow incorporating a large variety of argumentation theories, it is flexible enough to be applied to any type of dialogue. Since IAT relies on a standardized representation of arguments and argumentative structures, any argumentation theory schemes can be used to refine the analyses, and the reusability, revision and exchange of the IAT-analyzed dialogues is hence ensured.

This model is a philosophically grounded counterpart to the Argument Interchange Format (AIF) [CHE 06]. The developers of the AIF have tackled the problem of the existence of a wide variety of argumentation theories by proposing a standard way of representing argument analyses. The proposed format allows various theories to make use of the same language in their argument visualization tools, enabling the efficient interchange of data between tools for argument visualization and manipulation (e.g. [REE 17]).

In the AIF, claims are represented by Information nodes (I nodes), and the relationship between claims by Scheme Nodes (S-nodes): inference relations are represented by RA nodes and relations of conflict by CA nodes. An adjunct ontology, AIF+, was later developed to handle the representation of dialogical argumentation, in which the format of the dialogue structure mirrors the one of the argumentation structure [REE 08b]. Locution nodes (L nodes) capture speech acts and speakers, whereas Transition nodes (TA nodes) capture the relationship between L nodes.

IAT has been developed to capture the missing link between argument structures and dialogue structures: by taking into account the illocutionary force of utterances, IAT allows the representation of illocutionary structures that link L nodes to I nodes. Moreover, given that some speakers' communicative intentions cannot be determined without knowing the broader context of the dialogue – that is, what an utterance is responding to – IAT assumes that it is only by taking into account the relation between L nodes that some illocutionary forces can be inferred; as a result, these illocutionary schemes are anchored in TA nodes and can target I nodes or S nodes (to elicit inference or conflict relations between propositions) [BUD 16]. IAT is therefore a framework developed for the analysis of dialogues in order to elicit argumentative structures. By making the illocutionary forces of locutions apparent, the model allows identifying the argumentative dynamics generated by dialogical moves. The IAT graphical representations of dialogical structures and the attached illocutionary and argumentative structures represent a valuable framework for fine-grained analyses of discourse.

To sum up, an IAT analysis is composed of elements eliciting argument structures and dialogical dynamics via the representation of illocutionary connections, as summarized below:

– The right-hand side of a graph displays the dialogical structure with:

- L nodes: the content of the utterances preceded by the speaker's identification;

- TA nodes: the transitions between the locutions (or rules of dialogue)[4].

– The left-hand side of a graph displays the argumentative structure with:

- I nodes: the propositional content of each locution (in front of the corresponding locution node);

- relations of inference (RA nodes): they connect premises to conclusions;

- relations of conflict (CA nodes): they connect conflicting information nodes;

- relations of rephrase (MA nodes): when two information nodes mean the same despite different propositional contents or linguistic surface (see [KON 16]);

– The relation between the dialogical and the argumentative structure:

- illocutionary forces connecting a locution node to the corresponding information node (c.g. asserting, questioning and challenging);

- illocutionary forces connecting a transition node to scheme node (i.e. that can only be derived from the transitions between locutions; e.g. arguing and disagreeing);

- indexical illocutionary forces connecting a transition node to an information node (e.g. challenging and agreeing)[5].

Let us consider the simple example below, taken from the MM2012c corpus[6], and describe its IAT analysis in Figure 6.7. The dialogue below (transcribed from a Moral Maze episode) involves Melanie, a panelist, and Alexander, a witness, who are talking about the morality of letting the state interfere in dysfunctional families.

> Alexander Brown: *If you're pointing to the phenomena of multiple or clustered disadvantage, if I were going to name one form of disadvantage as the key determiner it would be poverty, not lack of marriage.*
>
> Melanie Philips: *Why?*
>
> Alexander Brown: *Because evidence shows that those who are in poverty are more likely to be facing all of these other forms of disadvantage.*

---

4 In a dialogue, locutions are the moves that speakers make. The rules of the dialogue should constrain speakers to advance certain types of moves and prevent them to advance others at some point in the dialogue. Transition nodes capture the concept of *rules of dialogue* by eliciting the relationship between locutions, that is, which rule has been triggered that allows a speaker to respond to another speaker, for example. This concept of *rule of dialogue* is visible in dialectical games, in which rules explicitly define the rights and obligations of speakers.

5 IAT can also handle reported speech by unpacking the propositional content of a reported speech and the propositional content of a reporting speech.

6 More details about this corpus are given in section 6.5.9.

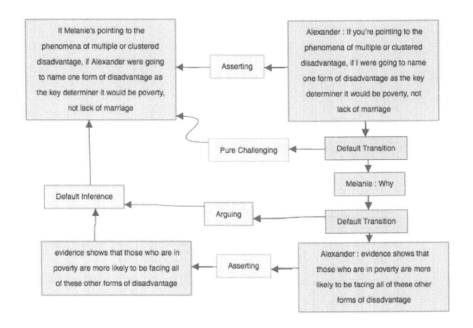

Figure 6.7. *An IAT analysis. For a color version of this figure, see www.iste.co.uk/janier/argument.zip*

On the right-hand side in Figure 6.7, one can see the dialogical structure, with the speakers' locutions and the transitions between locutions that represent the dialogical relevance of moves, represented by Default Transition nodes.

The left-hand side of the figure represents the argumentative structure: the proposition *if Melanie's pointing to the phenomena of multiple or clustered disadvantage, if Alexander were going to name one form of disadvantage as the key determiner it would be poverty, not lack of marriage* is inferentially related to *evidence shows that those who are in poverty are more likely to be facing all of these other forms of disadvantage*; this is represented by the Default Inference node. This means that the first proposition is the conclusion and it is supported by one premise.

6.2.4. *Summary*

The three models presented above show that argument annotation can take many different forms since they do not aim at studying the same aspects of argumentation. We consider these models as relevant and well-known frameworks, although many other models exist, which bear their own capacities and quality.

An important facet of argument annotation is that it is not only a complex task but it is overall time consuming: for instance, I. Habernal and I. Gurevych [HAB 17] explain that it took on average 35 h for each of their three analysts to annotate their data with five categories only. The reader can refer to [BUD 18] or [HAB 17] for detailed reports on annotation processes.

6.3. Guidelines for argument analysis

Keeping in mind that the annotation process is only a first step toward argument mining, the annotations must be consistent with what the argument mining system is designed to do. Moreover, in order to train a system for automatic argument mining, annotations must be reliable. To ensure accuracy and reliability, it is necessary to have several annotators analyzing the same text, but analyzing argumentation is a rather subjective task; variability between annotators is therefore common. This represents a major drawback since argument mining systems may infer patterns from contradictory evidence. To reduce subjectivity and ensure consistency, guidelines for annotators are needed. Different methodologies exist for the definition of guidelines, as we will show here.

6.3.1. *Principles of annotation guidelines*

In order to ensure the reproducibility of annotations by several annotators, the concepts involved need to be delimited, an annotation protocol needs to be established and human annotators must be trained. Annotation guidelines serve these purposes: they establish a method for the detection and annotation of argument structures and components. They can also be used as a documentation for the resulting annotated data: people who want to use these resources can read annotation guidelines to better understand the semantics of the annotations at stake. In other words, publicly releasing guidelines helps future annotators and readers of an argument analysis. Some researchers have therefore published their annotation handbooks; see, for instance, [STA 15, SAU 06, VIS 18]. Usually, the protocol for an annotation effort mainly consists of the following steps:

1) read and understand the text as a whole, to properly assess its communicative aims, to understand the context of each argument component;

2) identify the main claims of the argumentation;

3) identify claims, premises, attacks;

4) identify missing components (e.g. implicit claims, warrants, etc). This step can be skipped if the annotation aim is to analyze explicit argument components only;

5) label argument components according to the inventory for the annotation effort at stake;

6) identify relations between argument components or identify bigger argumentative structures integrating argument components.

Note that in annotation guidelines, it is important to include typical examples for each step in order to provide annotators with concrete instantiations.

6.3.2. *Inter-annotator agreements*

Since annotations correspond to annotators' judgments, there is not an objective way of establishing the validity of an annotation. But a metric about how certain one is of the annotations must be provided; this is called the Inter-Annotator Agreement (IAA). An IAA indeed shows:

– how easy it was to clearly delineate the categories: if the annotators make the same decision in almost all cases, then the annotation guidelines were very *clear*;

– how *trustworthy* the annotation is: if the IAA is low, it is because the annotators found it difficult to agree on which items belong to which category;

– how reliable the annotation is: annotations are reliable if annotators consistently make the same decisions; this proves the *validity*;

– how *stable* the annotation is: the extent to which an annotator will produce the same classifications. Stability can be investigated by calculating agreement for the same annotator over time;

– how *reproducible* the annotation is: the extent to which different annotators will produce the same classification; reproducibility can be investigated by calculating agreement for different annotators.

There are different ways and metrics for calculating the IAA; we provide some such metrics below. This evaluation step is mandatory to ensure that the annotations are accurate and reproducible.

1) *The Measure of Observed Agreement* gives the percentage of annotations on which the annotators agree:

$$\frac{Number\ Of\ Items\ On\ Which\ Annotators\ Agree}{Total\ Number\ Of\ Items}$$

This approach is seen as biased because it does not take into account the agreement that is due by chance (i.e. when annotators make random choices). Therefore, it is not a good measure of reliability.

2) *Cohen's kappa (κ)* measures the agreement between two annotators who classify N items into C mutually exclusive categories.

Note that this κ measures agreement between *two* annotators only. Contrary to the Measure of Observed Agreement, Cohen's kappa takes into account how often annotators are expected to agree if they make random choices.

The equation for Cohen's κ is:

$$\kappa = \frac{\Pr(a) - \Pr(e)}{1 - \Pr(e)}$$

where $\Pr(a)$ is the relative observed agreement among annotators and $\Pr(e)$ is the hypothetical probability of chance agreement, using the observed data to calculate the probabilities of each observer randomly assigning each category. If the annotators are in complete agreement, then $\kappa = 1$. If there is no agreement among them other than what would be expected by chance (as defined by $\Pr(e)$), then $\kappa = 0$.

3) *Fleiss's kappa (κ)* [FLE 71] is a statistical measure for assessing the reliability of agreement between a fixed number of annotators when assigning categories to a fixed number of items. This contrasts with other kappas such as Cohen's κ, which only works when assessing the agreement between two annotators.

The kappa, κ, can be defined as,

$$\kappa = \frac{\bar{P} - \bar{P}_e}{1 - \bar{P}_e}$$

The factor $1 - \bar{P}_e$ gives the degree of agreement that is attainable above chance, and $\bar{P} - \bar{P}_e$ gives the degree of agreement actually achieved above chance. If the annotators are in complete agreement, then $\kappa = 1$. If there is no agreement among the raters (other than what would be expected by chance), then $\kappa \leq 0$.

4) *Krippendorff's alpha (α)* [KRI 04] is the most reliable, but the most difficult measure. Unlike Cohen's and Fleiss's statistics, which measure observed and expected agreement, Krippendorff's equation measures observed *and* expected disagreement.

Krippendorff's α is applicable to any number of coders, each assigning one value to one unit of analysis. Software for calculating Krippendorff's α is available at http://web.asc.upenn.edu/usr/krippendorff/dogs.html.

6.3.3. *Interpretation of IAA measures*

Measuring the IAA allows to identify weaknesses in an annotation effort but also in a model or in the guidelines. Indeed, when disagreements are observed between annotators, it is possible to refine the guidelines to avoid discrepancies afterwards. It is unlikely, however, that annotators never disagree on an annotation despite clear and stable guidelines. As a result, the IAA results influence the decision to use analyzed data as a development or training corpus at the time of designing an argument mining system.

J.R. Landis and G.G. Koch [LAN 77] considered the agreement between more than two annotators in the context of a clinical diagnosis. They supplied no evidence to support their interpretation; instead it is based on personal opinion. Table 6.1 presents their interpretation.

Results	Interpretations
0.0–0.2	Slight
0.2–0.4	Fair
0.4–0.6	Moderate
0.6–0.8	Substantial
0.8–1	Perfect

Table 6.1. *Interpretation of κ results, according to [LAN 77]*

Following their interpretation, a $\kappa \geq 0.8$ means that the annotations are stable, reliable and reproducible. Consequently, any annotation task resulting in an IAA inferior to 0.8 should not be considered as reliable; it would otherwise deliver poor results at the time of automatically reproducing the task via an argument mining system.

6.3.4. *Some examples of IAAs*

In order to prove the accuracy of their annotations, researchers can provide the results of the IAA. Generally, results tend to be higher when annotations are carried out on delimited domains, with detailed and specific guidelines. We provide here some results found in the literature:

– [ALK 16] obtain Fleiss's $\kappa = 0.56$ for the identification of argumentative components in a newspaper editorials corpus;

– [BIR 11] obtain $\kappa = 0.69$ for the identification of justifications to claims in blogs threads. In this case, an intensive use of the structure of the blog, in the form of restrictions for classification, allowed to maintain a substantial agreement. However, the authors did not release annotation guidelines;

– in [BUD 14b], two annotators analyzed argumentative dialogues with IAT (see section 6.2.3). They report a κ ranging from 0.75 for the detection of conflict relations to 0.9 for the analysis of illocutionary connections;

– [FAU 14] report $\kappa = 0.70$ for three annotators who analyzed 8,179 sentences from student essays and had to decide whether a given sentence provided reasons for or against the essay's major claim. In this annotation process, the author relied on Amazon Mechanical Turk;

– [PAR 14] obtain $\kappa = 0.73$ for the classification of propositions in four classes for 10,000 sentences in a public platform to discuss regulations (1,047 documents). In this narrow domain, the authors have clearly defined classes, which trigger good IAA results;

– [ROS 12] obtain $\kappa = 0.50$ for the detection of opinionated claims in 2,000 sentences of online discussions and $\kappa = 0.56$ for claims in 2,000 sentences from Wikipedia. Although classes are few, they are vaguely defined, and the domain allows for a wide range of variation;

– [SCH 13] obtain $\kappa = 0.48$ for the detection of argument schemes in discussions of deletions in Wikipedia discussion pages. As the authors state, the targeted annotation (argument schemes) is very complex, which makes agreement difficult;

– for their task of detecting argumentation (claims, major claims, premises and their relations) in 90 argumentative essays (ca. 30,000 tokens), in [STA 14], the authors report a Krippendorff's $\alpha U = 0.72$ for argument components and $\alpha = 0.81$ for relations between components. In this project, annotation guidelines are highly detailed and annotators extensively trained;

– [TEU 99b] obtains Fleiss' $\kappa = 0.71$ for an application to the domain of scientific articles. Here, classes are very specific and clearly defined by their function in the document.

6.3.5. *Summary*

We have seen that guidelines are used to train expert annotators. The sample of results presented in section 6.3.2 teaches us that, in order to end up with stable, valid and reproducible analyses, (1) guidelines for annotations must be clear and explicit, supported by definitions and examples and (2) analyses must be carried out by various annotators in order to discuss points on which consensus is not reached and improve guidelines. However, given that large amounts of data are needed to deliver a stable and efficient system, some have turned toward non-expert human annotators; see, for instance, [HAB 14, NGU 17]. Crowd-sourced annotations present an indisputable advantage; they allow the rapid gathering of large amounts of analyses. Nevertheless, crowd-sourcing also represents a massive drawback: non-experts, albeit provided with guidelines, tend to deliver poor results, as shown in [HAB 14]. It is therefore recommended to crowd-source annotations for tasks with clear and easy to understand guidelines.

As argued in [WAC 14], κ and α metrics do not show what parts of a text are easier or harder to annotate. Following their annotation work of ADUs in blog posts, they propose a new metrics: a clustering approach to quantify the agreement of annotators not only for the whole annotated text, but also for a given text segment. Equally, K. Budzynska *et al.* [BUD 18] created a corpus of annotated dialogical arguments without using a traditional method for IAA. Their project was to analyze a debate in a very constrained period of time which left no time for evaluation. Their method is built on two approaches: (1) the iterative enhancement, which consists in iterating annotations after semiautomatic techniques are applied to reveal inconsistencies and (2) the agile corpus creation, where annotations are carried out following a step-by-step process. To do so, they recruited eight experienced annotators (i.e. who had prior knowledge of the annotation scheme) and 10 non-expert annotators who have been trained on a very short time. For this, guidelines for the annotation were proposed and are publicly available[7]. Throughout the annotation process, experienced annotators discussed the analyses with non-expert ones in order to assess the quality of the annotations and quickly verified the analyses with a checklist referencing the most common mistakes.

In conclusion, annotations of argumentative texts take various forms and do not yield the same results depending on the annotation tasks. It is however necessary to have reliable annotated data to ensure a consistent argument mining system afterwards.

6.4. Annotation tools

Annotating arguments with the aim of providing with a consistent argument mining system requires the annotations to be computationally tractable. Hence, it is necessary to use computational or web-based tools for the annotation task.

Some such tools have not primarily been designed for argument annotations but can, nevertheless, be used for such a task. On the other hand, some annotation tools have specifically been developed for argument analyses. We present here several graphical interfaces that can be used for the annotation task, along with their advantages and drawbacks.

6.4.1. *Brat*

Brat is an online environment for collaborative text annotation. It is designed for structured annotations, which means that it is possible to annotate text spans and then to show and name the links between several units [STE 12].

Although Brat is not specifically designed for argument analysis, it has been used in several works for the annotation of arguments [LIE 16, TER 18]. Brat, indeed, enables users to add their own scheme set. It is available at http://brat.nlplab.org.

---

7 http://arg-tech.org/IAT-guidelines.

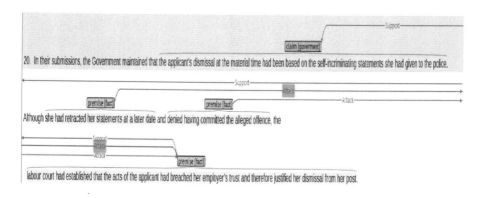

Figure 6.8. *An argument analysis in Brat. For a color version of this figure, see www.iste.co.uk/janier/argument.zip*

Figure 6.8 shows an argument analysis performed in Brat. In this analysis, ADUs have been assigned a category (*claim* or *premise*). Relationships between these units have been described too (*support* or *attack*), providing a detailed analysis.

Long-distance dependencies create complex analyses; the linear presentation of the analyses made with Brat represents a major drawback, hampering their readability in some contexts: the structure of the arguments is not always clearly visualized and the connections between argument elements is sometimes difficult to follow. Brat can however suit some annotators, in particular for small texts or when few labels are needed.

6.4.2. *RST tool*

RST tool is a graphical interface for the annotation of text structures [ODO 00]. As we have seen in section 6.2.1, RST was not initially intended for the analysis of arguments but several works rely on RST relational power for the analysis of argumentation. RST tool allows to manually segment and annotate the relation between segments of a text. As in Brat, new schemes can be added (such as relations other than the initial RST relations). An interesting feature of RST tool is the possibility to extract descriptive statistics from each analysis. The interface also allows users to save, load, reuse and share analyses. The tool and a user guide are freely available at http://wagsoft.com/RSTTool.

Figure 6.9 shows the analysis of the text below (both taken from [PEL 13, p. 16]). It shows, for instance, that the two segments *We should tear the building down* and *because it is full of asbestos* are linked by a relation of *Evidence*:

We should tear the building down, because it is full of asbestos. In principle, it is possible to clean it up, but according to the mayor that would be forbiddingly expensive.

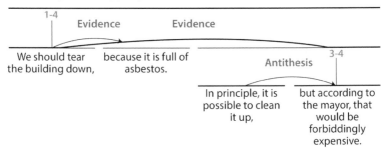

Figure 6.9. *An argument analysis with RST tool. For a color version of this figure, see www.iste.co.uk/janier/argument.zip*

6.4.3. *AGORA-net*

AGORA-net is a free computer-supported collaborative argument visualization tool (see http://agora.gatech.edu). It allows showing claims and premises as well as counterarguments. In an AGORA-net analysis, main claims are located on the top left of the map and premises on the right. AGORA-net has mainly been used in problem-solving contexts [HOF 15]. An example of argument analysis (taken from [HOF 14]) is given in Figure 6.10. It shows the main claim and the premises (in blue) as well as a counterargument (here *objection* in orange).

6.4.4. *Araucaria*

Araucaria is a free software tool for annotating arguments [REE 04][8]. This diagramming tool supports convergent and linked arguments, enthymemes and refutations. As in Brat, new annotation schemes can be added to suit annotators. It also supports argumentation schemes. Arguments analyzed in Araucaria can be saved in the portable format "Argument Markup Language" (AML), which is a flexible language allowing, for instance, to populate a database.

In Araucaria, analyzed claims are represented by nodes and links between them can also be drawn (to show premise–conclusion relationships). Implicit elements can be added to the analyses, such as missing premises, the degree of confidence in a premise or the strength of the inference.

---

8 See http://araucaria.computing.dundee.ac.uk/doku.php.

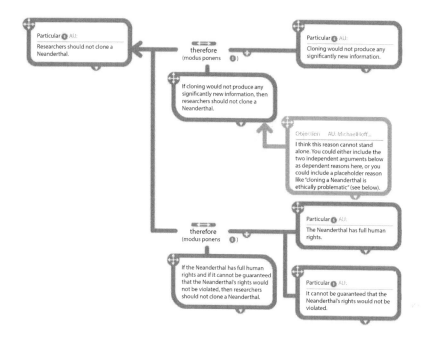

Figure 6.10. *An argument map with AGORA-net. For a color version of this figure, see www.iste.co.uk/janier/argument.zip*

Araucaria has been used in several works of research [MOE 07, MOC 09], in particular for the analysis of legal texts. Figure 6.11, taken from [REE 08a, p. 93], presents an analysis made in Araucaria. We can see that the tool allows showing premises and conclusions (plain nodes linked by arrows) and unexpressed claims (dashed nodes) as well as argument schemes.

6.4.5. *Rationale*

Rationale (http://rationaleonline.com) allows building argument maps in order to elicit argumentative structures. It has been developed to support students' critical thinking and writing skills. Rationale has extensively been used in the legal domain.

Figure 6.12, taken from [VAN 07, p. 26], shows an argument map created with Rationale. It shows the main claim (at the top) and the different premises (in green) and attacks (in red).

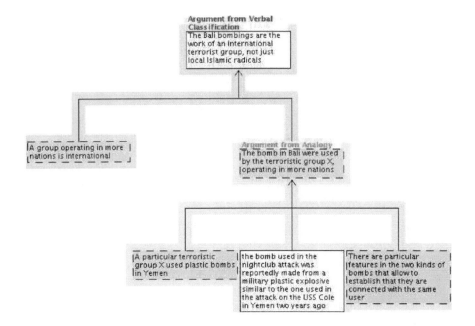

Figure 6.11. *An argument analysis in Araucaria. For a color version of this figure, see www.iste.co.uk/janier/argument.zip*

6.4.6. *OVA+*

OVA+ (Online Visualization of Argument) is an interface for the analysis of arguments online and is accessible from any web browser at http://ova.arg-tech.org. The tool was built as a response to the AIF [CHE 06]: it is a tool allowing what the AIF has advocated for, i.e. the representation of arguments and the possibility to exchange, share and reuse the argument maps. The system relies on IAT, a philosophically and linguistically grounded counterpart to the AIF [BUD 11] (see also section 6.2). The schemes provided allow for a graphical representation of the argumentative structure of a text, and more interestingly, dialogues [JAN 14].

At the end of the analysis, OVA+ permits saving the work on the user's computer as an image file. But the most interesting feature is the possibility of saving the analyses in the AIF format either locally or to AIFdb [LAW 12] and adding them to a dedicated corpus (created beforehand) in the AIFdb Corpora[9] (see section 6.5 for more details). Thus, the analyses can be reused via AIFdb or loaded in OVA+ for consultation or correction.

---

9 http://corpora.aifdb.org.

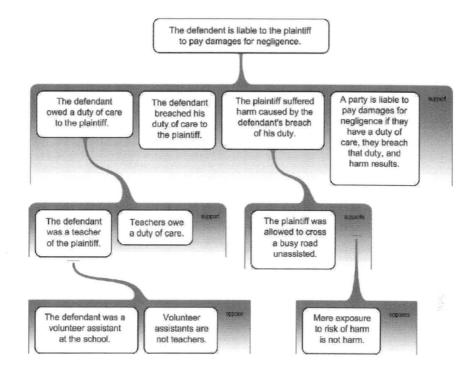

Figure 6.12. *An argument map with Rationale. For a color version of this figure, see www.iste.co.uk/janier/argument.zip*

Figure 6.13, taken from [REE 17, p. 146], is the analysis of an argumentative dialogue. It allows showing the dialogical dynamics (right-hand side of the figure) and the corresponding argumentative structure (on the left) via the analysis of illocutionary forces (here, asserting, challenging and arguing). OVA+ mainly relies on the IAT framework, therefore conflicts as well as rephrases can also be analyzed and represented.

Contrary to Brat for instance, OVA+, just like Araucaria, has been specifically designed for the analysis of argumentation, which makes the visualization of argumentative structures easier.

6.4.7. *Summary*

The six tools presented above have been designed for different purposes; as a result, they possess their own features, qualities and drawbacks. They are only a small sample of the various existing annotation tools. Other tools for annotating arguments in text exist, presenting different graphical representations, features or schemes; see, for instance, Dedoose (http://dedoose.com), Lite Map – previously Cohere (http://litemap.net) or Compendium (http://compendiuminstitute.org), to name just a few.

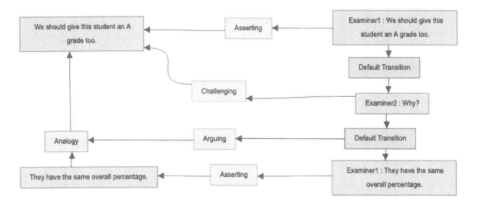

Figure 6.13. *An argument analysis in OVA+. For a color version of this figure, see www.iste.co.uk/janier/argument.zip*

6.5. Argument corpora

As argued in [HAB 17], the argumentation community lacks data for designing, training and evaluating argument mining algorithms. Scholars may need to build their own corpus, which can be challenging, in particular if the domain at stake involves sensitive data or ethical matters (see, for instance, [JAN 16]).

In order to illustrate their work but also to save others from the burden of finding and gathering texts to create a corpus, some researchers have gathered their analyzed data and made them available. However, they do not all contain the same type of data since they have been used for different objectives. As a result, already available corpora may not suit all argument annotation tasks and aims[10]. We propose here a sample of argument corpora, which have been built and shared by the community, along with some of their characteristics.

---

10 The annotation process being a highly demanding task, corpora to be annotated are sometimes preprocessed, for instance to presegment the text or simply to verify whether argumentation is present (see, for instance, [HAB 17]).

6.5.1. *COMARG*

The COMARG corpus was not built for argument mining but for opinion mining [BOL 14]: the argument structure is not what the authors intended to highlight; rather, their goal was to elicit the arguments used to support an opinion. The dataset comes from two discussion websites covering controversial topics. Each argument has been labeled by three trained annotators as either *for* or *against* the topic. The authors report a Cohen's $\kappa = 0.49$.

6.5.2. *A news editorial corpus*

K. Al-Khatib *et al.*[ALK 16] developed a corpus of 300 news editorials from online news portals annotated with domain-dependent units that synthesize the role of a portion of text within the document as a whole (e.g. *common ground*, *assumption* or *anecdote*). Each editorial was annotated by three annotators, with an overall IAA of Fleiss's $\kappa = 0.56$.

6.5.3. *THF Airport ArgMining corpus*

This corpus, which has been used to train an argument mining system, gathers annotations of contributions to an online discussion platform in German. The analyses have been performed in Brat (see section 6.4.1) for the detection of *major positions*, *claims* and *premises* [LIE 16]. The reader can visit http://dbs.cs.uni-duesseldorf.de/datasets/argmining to consult the THF Airport ArgMining corpus.

6.5.4. *A Wikipedia articles corpus*

E. Aharoni *et al.* [AHA 14] propose a corpus of annotated *claims* and their corresponding *evidence* of 586 Wikipedia articles. The authors report a Cohen's $\kappa = 0.39$ and $\kappa = 0.40$ for the analyses of claims and evidence, respectively. The corpus is available upon request.

6.5.5. *AraucariaDB*

The Araucaria corpus [REE 06] is a corpus of annotated texts (from a variety of sources and domains), realized in the Araucaria software (see section 6.4.4) and presenting *argument structures* and, more interestingly, *argument schemes*. Despite the relative subjectivity involved in differentiating argument schemes (see section 6.1.5), C. Reed [REE 06] notes that some argumentation schemes occur frequently in the corpus. Thus, the Araucaria corpus has been used as a proof-of-concept for argument mining systems that aim to detect argumentation schemes (see [MOC 09, FEN 11]). Unfortunately, annotation guidelines and IAAs have not been reported.

6.5.6. *An annotated essays corpus*

In their general purpose corpus, Stab and Gurevych [STA 14] have identified *claims, premises, support and attack relations*, with a $\kappa = 0.72$ for argument components and $\kappa = 0.81$ for relations. The domain of the corpus being quite general (argumentative essays), the argumentative strategies found in this kind of text are very general and it can be expected that they can be ported to other domains with little effort.

6.5.7. *A written dialogs corpus*

In [BIR 11], O. Biran and O. Rambow annotated *claims* and *justifications* in LiveJournal blog threads and Wikipedia pages. They do not provide guidelines but report a $\kappa = 0.69$.

6.5.8. *A web discourse corpus*

I. Habernal and I. Gurevych [HAB 17] claim to have built the largest corpus for argument mining purposes: it contains approximately 90,000 tokens from 340 documents. Additionally to various target domains (e.g. homeschooling or single-sex education), their corpus covers different genres such as online article comments, discussion forum posts or professional newswire articles. The reader can see section 6.2.2 for more details on the annotations.

6.5.9. *Argument Interchange Format Database*

AIFdb [11] is one of the largest datasets of annotated arguments[12]. In order to group argument maps and enable the search for maps that are related to each other, J. Lawrence *et al.* [LAW 15] propose the AIFdb Corpora interface[13], which allows users to create and share their corpora. AIFdb Corpora is closely related with OVA+ (see section 6.4.6); the interface therefore allows the creation of large corpora compliant with both AIF and IAT (see section 6.2.3). The argument maps thus elicit *argument and dialogue structures, argument schemes, illocutionary connections,*

---

11 http://aifdb.org.

12 In 2015, AIFdb contained over 4,000 argument maps [LAW 15].

13 http://corpora.aifdb.org.

among others (see sections 6.4.6 and 6.2.3 for an overview of the analytical framework).

AIFdb Corpora is actually a corpus of several corpora, coming from a wide range of sources (e.g. radio debates, mediation sessions, public consultations and political debates). Although this repository contains already analyzed argument structures (i.e. non-argumentative units are not presented), in some cases the original texts they are extracted from are also given. The tool also allows a user to share a link to their corpus and to view and download the corpus contents in different formats (SVG, PNG, DOT, JSON, RDF-XML, Prolog, as well as the format of the Carneades [BEX 12] and Rationale (see section 6.4.5) tools, or as an archive file containing JSON format representations of each argument map). It is also possible to view, evaluate and edit the argument maps contained within the corpus via OVA+.

Another interesting feature provided by the interface is its link to http://analytics.arg.tech; this offers statistics and insight into the size and structure of corpora, and allows comparison between them (for measuring a κ for instance) [REE 17].

6.5.10. *Summary*

Unsurprisingly, most corpora constructed so far concern the English language but a few other languages have also been considered. For instance, in AIFdb 11 languages are represented [LAW 15]; C. Houy *et al.* [HOU 13] and A. Peldszus [PEL 14] propose different corpora of German texts, whereas C. Sardianos *et al.* [SAR 15] and P. Reisert *et al.* [REI 14] present corpora of texts in Greek and Japanese languages, respectively.

This brief presentation of some corpora that have been built and shared is only a small sample of the different corpora used for argument annotations. This overview shows that data for argument detection and analysis are various: each corpus has its own characteristics and suits a specific aim. Despite a predominance of ad hoc corpora (meaning that they have been constructed for one particular purpose and, often, for one precise domain), some have been used to test models other than the one they had been built for in the first place. This shows that different frameworks and datasets can be valuable to different purposes. As an example, M. Lippi and P. Torroni [LIP 15] propose different corpora of German texts, including C. Stab and I. Gurevych's [STA 15] corpus, to test their model for argument detection. Unfortunately, some corpora have not been made public, impeding their sharing and use by others.

6.6. Conclusion

In this chapter, we have seen that argument annotation is a very challenging task. Although it relies on the same principle (i.e. the identification and analysis of argumentative components), not all existing frameworks for argument annotations focus on the same elements. We have also seen that precise guidelines are necessary to reach acceptable annotations, and the different tools that have been designed for argument analyses further demonstrate that the analysis of arguments can take various forms and not all argument analysis frameworks focus on the same facets of argumentation.

However, one can find, adapt or design the existing tools and frameworks to suit her needs. Moreover, the large range of corpora proposed in the literature shows that the diverse datasets for argument analysis have their own characteristics and each may suit upcoming research threads. Nevertheless, it can be argued that a reference corpus for argument mining would relieve scholars of the burden of building, annotating and evaluating such textual data, and would unify approaches. It must be kept in mind, however, that such a corpus would require a clear and detailed scheme along with reliable annotations. In the following chapter, we will show how manual analyses help building argument mining systems.

7

Argument Mining Applications
and Systems

There have been a large number of approaches to automated argument mining. The mainstream approach consists in applying machine learning (ML) techniques on manually annotated corpora to obtain a tool which automatically identifies argument structure in texts. In these cases, a corpus and its annotations determine the capabilities of the resulting tool. As an alternative to ML, some tools have been developed that rely on hand-crafted rules. For example, J. Kang and P. Saint-Dizier [KAN 14] present a discourse grammar implemented as a set of rules and constraints.

In this chapter, we present some systems that have been developed to automatically recognize the argumentative structure and the arguments in texts and to classify the detected arguments according to their type (e.g. counterarguments, rebuttals).

7.1. Application domains for argument mining

Argument mining serves the purpose of identifying *why* a speaker/writer holds such opinion. Some argument mining systems aim at describing argumentation (i.e. simply discovering arguments and, possibly, the relationships between several arguments), while another application of argument mining is to evaluate arguments (i.e. determining whether they are sound or to assess their influence in decisions). The most obvious application for argument mining systems is the analysis of the argumentative structure of a text (whether it is written or transcribed from oral data) to find the conclusion and the supporting or attacking elements for it [LIP 15]. Such analyses can have a further target in order to provide practical applications as we will see below.

Application domains for argument mining are varied. We list here some applications, contexts and fields that can benefit (or have benefited) from advances in argument mining. The aim here is not to provide an exhaustive list of the domains of applications but to present some of the possible fields of application and some tasks related to argument mining.

7.1.1. *Opinion analysis augmented by argument mining*

Knowing whether one is for or against, or whether one likes or dislikes something is the goal of opinion mining. But a deeper analysis may involve discovering *why* one holds an opinion. Argument mining tools can be applied to product reviews, for instance, in order to offer a company's marketing department the possibility to know the reasons why customers appreciate (or not) a product or service [SCH 12]. Another domain of application would be deliberation or politics because decision makers can learn more about citizens' opinions and expectations.

7.1.2. *Summarization*

Summarization consists in reducing a text to its main argument components (or highlighting them) [BAR 16] (see also section 4.3). It can be useful in many domains such as the legal and medical fields or for grasping the gist of a debate.

7.1.3. *Essays*

Persuasive essays are texts in which an author takes a stand on a topic and tries to convince readers. They therefore contain many arguments, which seems a natural choice for argument mining because essays are structured texts [STA 17].

7.1.4. *Dialogues*

Dialogues are another application domain for argument mining: people sharing their opinion may use arguments to convince their interlocutor(s) and may successfully do so. Whether they take place online (e.g. e-debates, online comments or Tweets) or orally (e.g. debates or discussions), dialogues present an additional challenge for argument mining since they are less constrained and many arguments are often more interrelated than in written contexts [BUD 14a].

7.1.5. *Scientific and news articles*

Scientific articles are texts containing arguments either to defend the author's position or to refute another author's stance or else to contrast several works. Scientific articles are above all argumentative since an author presenting her findings needs to explain why these findings are important. Discovering argumentation in scientific papers can help, for instance, to summarize findings [TEU 02].

News articles are argumentative texts too, in which an author presents a fact and can provide arguments. As in scientific articles, in this case the argumentation is usually clear and well performed since readers must follow and understand the author's stance and explanations.

7.1.6. *The Web*

The Web provides an immense source of arguments: people use web technologies to discuss topics, provide their opinions and comment on others'. This environment probably represents the biggest venue for argumentative natural language. Scholars have seen in this rich environment the opportunity to easily find arguments performed in an unconstrained manner even though it represents a huge challenge for argumentation mining [HAB 17].

7.1.7. *Legal field*

The development of argument mining systems was mainly initiated in the legal domain, surely because of its obvious argumentative character and rather constrained discourse, somehow easing the argument mining task [MOE 07]. Argument mining applications can be used to retrieve old cases in order to automatically find precedents for a current case, for example.

7.1.8. *Medical field*

The medical field is attracting attention, for instance, to detect the relation between symptoms and diseases [BOJ 01]. Applying argument mining to the medical field can save time for healthcare practitioners, for instance, by providing them with a summary of a patient's case or by automatically supplying them with a set of similar cases, which can help in establishing a protocol or rapidly diagnosing a condition.

7.1.9. *Education*

Argument mining can be adapted to the education field. Student essays, for instance, are usually structured texts; this provides the opportunity to easily detect argumentation. Indeed, to structure their essays, students use discourse connectives or even titles that can help to detect arguments and/or to determine the argumentative structures [FAU 14]. Applying argument mining systems to education may support the automatic correction and marking of students' works.

7.2. Principles of argument mining systems

There are two main approaches to automatic argument mining: rule- and corpus-based approaches. In rule-based systems, an expert writes rules to identify and interpret arguments. These systems tend to be accurate, mostly if they belong to a limited domain, but have low coverage. On the other hand, corpus-based systems are inferred by ML from examples that have been analyzed by annotators. These systems can have low accuracy but tend to have bigger coverage, especially if the number of examples is big enough or the strategies to generalize from examples are adequate. It can be expected that an automated approach, be it rule-based or ML, performs well in cases where annotators have a higher agreement (see section 6.3.2).

As [LIP 16] summarize it, every argument mining system has its own granularity (i.e. the level of detail at which arguments are searched: sentences, paragraphs, etc.), genre (dialogues, news, etc.), target (e.g. detection of claims or of premise/conclusion relations) and goal (e.g. detection and classification). Just like manual analyses of arguments, argument mining systems encompass several interrelated tasks. Argument mining systems, therefore, tend to follow the same principles and carry out subtasks step by step. Most systems developed so far rely on a pipeline architecture, meaning that the original, unstructured texts are gradually processed to eventually produce a structured document showing the detected arguments and (possibly) their components. This pipeline is summarized in Figure 7.1 (see also section 5.4). The output generally takes shape of an argument graph. Note that the automatic analysis of machines fails mostly in the same issues where humans have a lower agreement. However, humans perform consistently better than automated procedures when knowledge, reasoning and common sense are involved, without shallow cues like discourse markers.

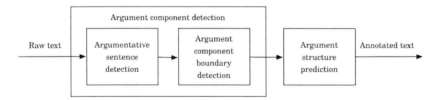

Figure 7.1. *The argument mining pipeline*

We summarize here the different stages of an argument mining exercise, along with some machine learning (ML) and natural language processing (NLP) techniques, which can be used to perform each task.

7.2.1. *Argumentative discourse units detection*

The first typical stage of argument mining is to delimit text spans that could constitute claims. Then, sentences that have a debatable character must be identified. This step corresponds to the detection of argumentative discourse units (ADUs) during manual analyses of arguments; it is as complex for a computational system as for a human annotator to distinguish sentences with an argumentative function from the ones that are non-argumentative (see section 6.1). For this reason, in some systems, input texts are segmented prior to being processed [STA 14]. *Linguistic cues* can provide useful information to determine whether a text span is argumentative or not (e.g. scalar adjectives, verbs, adverbs or modals).

Classifiers are the most commonly used technique to distinguish argumentative units from the non-argumentative ones. Classifiers usually use *Bag of Words* representations; roughly, if a word that has been predefined as being typical of argumentative sentences is found in a text, the classifier will codify the unit as being argumentative. Argument mining systems can also rely on the following ML and NLP techniques:

– *text segmentation* [CHO 00];

– *sentence classification* [KIM 14];

– *question classification* [ZHA 03].

When the output of the argument mining process is an argument graph, ADUs take the form of nodes. See section 8.1 for more details on the detection of ADUs by argument mining systems.

7.2.2. *Units labeling*

Once ADUs have been detected, the next step is the labeling of units, that is, determining the role of each unit in the argumentation (e.g. determining whether a unit is a claim, a conclusion, a premise, etc.). At this stage, the argument components must be classified according to their type: claim, premise, conclusion, counterargument, etc. A few NLP and ML techniques can be applied to carry out this task:

– *sequence labeling* [NGU 07];

– *named entity recognition* [NAD 07].

Just like during manual annotations (see section 6.1), the unit labeling task depends on the purpose of the mining process and the theory at stake too: one may not be interested in identifying warrants, for example, and only focus on the detection of premises and conclusions (e.g. for product reviews).

7.2.3. *Argument structure detection*

The following step in the argument mining pipeline is the detection of the argument structure. In other words, the system must represent the links between the previously extracted and clearly identified (or labeled) ADUs. At this stage, the system must label the links according to their detected type, for example, conflict, rebuttal, cause, etc. As argued in [PEL 13], two types of relations are usually concerned here: *causal* ones (i.e. supports) and *contrastive* ones (i.e. conflicts).

While some links are easily detected by argument mining systems, others are much more challenging, not because the type of relation is hard to distinguish but because some syntactic constructions are inherently complex. Different NLP techniques are therefore applied. Let us take the following examples:

The vaccine is toxic because the adjuvant is toxic.

If a system has correctly segmented the text in two argumentative segments ("the vaccine is toxic" and "the adjuvant is toxic"), it may easily identify the relation between them via a *discourse relation classification* [LIN 09]: the connective *because* is a clear indication of causality. Let us now take the same example without the connective:

The vaccine is toxic. The adjuvant is toxic.

This time, the task of automatically identifying the relation between the segments may be trickier: the absence of explicit marker of causality (or *cue phrases*) is challenging. For a human annotator, this sentence may not be analyzed with difficulty if s/he has sufficient knowledge to know that adjuvants are used to produce vaccines. For a system, however, acquiring such knowledge is hard. An additional technique must therefore be put into place such as a *semantic textual similarity* classifier [ACH 08].

Situations in which argumentative support is not explicitly marked (as in the example above) are very frequent in texts. Conflicts, however, tend to be more clearly signalled, as it would be complicated for a reader to follow a text in which contrasting opinions are not explicitly marked. Hence, markers can be used as cues to automatically uncover conflicts. Nevertheless, the problem of detecting conflictual relations arises frequently in dialogues, where an opponent may not need to clearly state her disagreement (e.g. "I disagree with what you've just said") and, rather, will state a new (opposing) claim. If disagreements can be understood straightforwardly in a discussion, automatically detecting them is a whole different story.

Here are some NLP techniques that are usually applied:

– *textual entailment* [AND 10];

– *link prediction* [GET 05];

– *detection of verb tenses for temporal ordering of events* [MAN 03];

– *detection of word pairs in causal relations (e.g. fall-hurt)* [CHA 06].

Other relations exist beside supports and conflicts. As an example, while some works of research consider that examples are supports for claims (hence the *Argument from Example* argument scheme), others deem them to be a different type of argumentative relation. Similarly, while *restatements* can be considered as sheer repetitions (as in [PEL 13], who put the original argumentative unit and its restatement in one single node in the analytical diagrams), they can also be seen as having another role in the argumentation. For example, restatements may add to the force of an argument [KON 16].

Again, some relations may be of no interest for some projects. As an example, conflict relations may be left aside if the goal is simply to detect the main claim in a news article.

7.2.4. *Argument completion*

When elements of an argument do not appear in a text, they may need to be reconstructed. For instance, reconstructing enthymemes or inducing implicit warrants may be necessary to obtain the most complete argument possible [RAJ 16, SAI 18]. Reconstructing implicit arguments is a challenging task, though this step is not mandatory (for example, when one is only interested in what the text explicitly presents). Another interesting application of automatic argument completion is when one is interested in identifying the argument schemes: as we have seen in section 6.1.5, some elements of an argument scheme may not be explicitly stated but can be reconstructed.

7.2.5. *Argument structure representation*

After the argument component detection – and reconstruction – one may want to present the general argumentative structure of the analyzed text. The generated output is usually structured as a graph. The overall graphical representation obviously depends on the argument model (or framework), on which the system is based. If the model is only interested in premise/conclusion relationships, the formalization is therefore more straightforward than in models which go beyond such a link and try to elicit rebuttals and warrants, for example (see section 6.2).

Results of the automatic annotation of arguments and argument structures can also be presented in XML (Extended Markup Language), which is useful for the exchange of data between different programs and because it offers the possibility to clearly represent structures (such as tree structures).

7.3. **Some existing systems for argument mining**

In this section, we will present some existing argument mining systems. To the best of our knowledge, no system allows the automatic carrying out of all the tasks presented above: most of them only focus on the detection of claims but many intend to execute several ensuing tasks such as the structure detection task. Hitherto, argument mining systems deliver little accuracy but results tend to be better when the model and the domain of application are clearly delimited. As a result, ad hoc systems are often privileged. Indeed, when applying ML techniques on manually annotated corpora to obtain a tool that automatically identifies argument structure in texts, the corpus and the annotations totally determine the capabilities of the resulting tool. We list below some systems that have been developed in order to automatically detect arguments and/or argument structures.

7.3.1. *Automatic detection of rhetorical relations*

Such systems have been designed to automatically build RST trees – or tantamount structures (see section 6.1.8) – highlighting, for example, *cause* and *contrast* relations [MAR 99, MAR 02, BLA 07]. The main corpora that are used to train such systems are the RST Treebank and the Penn Discourse Treebank (PDTB) [MAR 02, HER 10, LIN 09]. Different methods (supervised or semisupervised) have been applied across the literature triggering various results.

O. Biran and O. Rambow [BIR 11] rely on four different corpora (Wikipedia pages, RST Treebank, blog threads from Live Journal and Wikipedia discussion pages) along the different stages of development of their model for the identification of *justifications*. They use a naive Bayes classifier (a supervised ML method) and reach F1-score = 39.35 for the Wikipedia discussion pages.

A. Peldszus and M. Stede [PEL 13] identify two major limitations to these systems, including that most works turn out to be oversimplistic because they only consider nucleus–satellite relations and do not identify more complex structures.

7.3.2. *Argument zoning*

Although argument zoning is not really argument mining, it can be considered as one of the cornerstones for argument mining processes. In [TEU 99a], the author has worked on scientific papers and proposed a way of automatically detecting *zones* within them and range them into seven categories:

– *Aim*: the goal of the paper;

– *Textual*: statements indicating the sections structure;

– *Background*: generally accepted scientific background;

– *Own*: statement describing the author's work;

– *Contrast*: when the author compares the current work with others';

– *Basis*: statements showing agreement with other works;

– *Other*: when the author describes others' works.

The author has used a naive-Bayes approach for the automatic classification triggering very good results for the category *Own* (86%) but only 26% for the *Contrast* category.

7.3.3. Stance detection

In [GOT 14], the authors limit themselves to the prediction of *stance*, i.e. the attitude of an author/speaker toward a subject: the author of a text (here, posts in Debatepedia) can be *for* or *against* a given topic. The authors used sentiment lexicons and named entity recognition and achieved accuracy around 0.80. Although this work relates more to sentiment mining, it can be considered as a first step toward argument mining.

7.3.4. Argument mining for persuasive essays

In [STA 17], the authors propose a model for identifying argument components (*major claims*, *claims* and *premises*) and detecting *argumentation structures* in texts coming from an online forum where users provide correction and feedback about other users' research papers, essays or poetry. Their model also differentiates between *support* and *attack* relations. They obtain 95.2% of human performance for component identification, 87.9% for argumentation structures detection and 80.5% for support and attack relations. This pipeline model is one of the first approaches that allows identifying the global argument structure of texts.

7.3.5. Argument mining for web discourse

I. Habernal and I. Gurevych [HAB 17] have created an experimental software for argumentation mining in user-generated web content. Their system is under free license and available at http://kp.tu-darmstadt.de/data/argumentation-mining. The authors identify *argument components* in web discourse (with a large variety of registers and domains) using Structural Support Vector Machine (SVM) and a sequence labeling approach reaching an overall Macro-F1 = 0.251.

The authors of [CAB 12] worked on 19 topics from Debatepedia (online dialogical texts) and used existing research on textual entailment (the off-the-shelf EDITS system) and argumentation theory to extract *arguments* and evaluate their *acceptability*. They achieved an F1 score of 0.75.

7.3.6. *Argument mining for social media*

C. Llewellyn *et al.* [LLE 14] and M. Dusmanu *et al.* [DUS 17] have developed systems specifically for the domain of social media (here, Twitter). Social media present many difficulties to be treated by standard NLP tools: language, in particular, has many deviations from standard usage.

In [LLE 14], the authors classified *claims, counterclaims, verification inquiries* and *comments* from tweets, using supervised ML techniques such as unigrams, punctuation, Part of Speech (POS), naive Bayes, SVM and decision trees. They obtain an agreement between human and automatic annotations ranging from $\kappa = 0.26$ to $\kappa = 0.86$.

For the distinction between *factual and opiniated tweets*, M. Dusmanu *et al.* [DUS 17] apply classification algorithms (Logistic Regression and Random Forest) and obtain an F1 measure of 0.78 for argument versus non-argument classification.

T. Goudas *et al.* [GOU 14] carry out claim/premise mining in social media texts. They identified *argumentative sentences* with F1 = 0.77, using the Maximum Entropy (ME) classifier. To identify *premises*, they used BIO encoding of tokens and achieved an F1 score of 0.42 using conditional random fields (CRFs).

7.3.7. *Argument scheme classification and enthymemes reconstruction*

V. Feng and G. Hirst [FEN 11] have built a system for the automatic classification of five *argument schemes* (as defined in [WAL 08]): practical reasoning, arguments from example, from consequence, from cause to effect and from verbal classification. The final goal of their approach is the reconstruction of *enthymemes*.

This work has made use of the Araucaria corpus, saving the authors from the burden of discarding non-argumentative units and identifying premises and conclusions. Their system attains up to 98% accuracy in differentiating between scheme pairs.

7.3.8. *Argument classes and argument strength classification*

J. Park and C. Cardie [PAR 14] used SVM and other features such as n-grams, POS or sentiment clue words to classify propositions from online user comments into three classes: *unverifiable, verifiable non-experimental,* and *verifiable experimental.* The classification then allows to provide an estimate of how adequately the arguments have been supported (i.e. whether the arguments are strong). In their work, they ignored non-argumentative texts and achieved MacroF1 = 68.99%.

7.3.9. *Textcoop*

Textcoop[1] is a platform that uses grammars for discourse processing and automatic annotation of various linguistic features. It has been used to annotate different types and genres of texts such as procedural texts [SAI 12], debates [BUD 14b], as well as opiniated texts such as user reviews [VIL 12]. The system allows the detection of *conclusions* (main claims), *supports* and *argument strength.* This rule-based system also allows detecting structures that go beyond the claim–premise relation such as *specialization, definition* or *circumstance* [KAN 14].

Although the tool is not designed solely for argumentation, its use for the detection of argumentative structures and illocutionary forces (see section 6.2.3) has triggered satisfactory results, for example, [BUD 14b] indicates that the system correctly identified 85% of ADUs and 78% of illocutionary connections.

7.3.10. *IBM debating technologies*

The largest argument mining dataset to date is currently being developed at IBM Research[2] (see also [AHA 14]). In [RIN 15], the authors developed a system for automatically detecting *evidences* from text that support a given *claim.* This task finds several practical applications in decision support and persuasion enhancement, for instance.

7.3.11. *Argument mining for legal texts*

R. Mochales Palau and M.-F. Moens [MOC 09] have worked on the ECHR corpus (see section 6.5) and implemented ML techniques (rather than linguistic features) for the detection of *arguments* via a naive Bayes classifier and obtain 73% accuracy. Their system also allows classifying argumentative units as either *premises* or *conclusions* with good results: 68.12% for the detection of premises and 74.07% for conclusions. Finally, their system permits the detection of argumentative structures (i.e. how argumentative units relate to each other) and obtain 60% accuracy.

---

1 The system is available from the authors upon request.

2 http://researcher.watson.ibm.com/researcher/view_group.php?id=5443.

7.4. Efficiency and limitations of existing argument mining systems

The first issue with argument mining is the inherent complexity of the task that makes the development of such systems very difficult and time consuming. Hence, most systems described in the literature are often evaluated on small datasets; as a consequence, results must be cautiously judged.

Given the various approaches to argument mining that exist and the different goals of the systems developed so far, it would be meaningless to try and compare them and their results. However, authors reporting on their systems' results tend to agree on the tasks that yield satisfactory results and the ones that need further improvements. Thus, R. Mochales Palau and M.-F. Moens [MOC 09] report an accuracy of 73% for ADUs detection and Budzynska *et al.* [BUD 14b] report an accuracy of 85%. The classification of units – as claims, premises or conclusions, for instance – yields very different results, as we have seen in section 7.3. The relation detection task, in turn, does not seem to return that much divergent results: R. Mochales Palau and M.-F. Moens [MOC 09] obtain 60% and C. Stab and I. Gurevych [STA 17] reach 87.9%.

The difference in the results between the models also comes from the fact not all authors agree on the definition of the various argument components and use different techniques for automatically detecting them. Indeed, each argument mining system has been designed for a specific genre and goal. Furthermore, rule-based systems tend to be more accurate than corpus-based systems (which rely on ML techniques) but the domain of application has to be clearly delimited. To the most of our knowledge, no system has been constructed with a general-purpose spirit; this is obviously understandable given the complexity of the task. But efforts in that direction have to be made. One step in that direction would be the opportunity to share corpora and annotation schemes between systems. For example, different models rely on the same corpora for different purposes. This proves that a corpus for argument mining tasks would be valuable to a wide community of researchers. A framework may allow this sharing and reusing of data and annotations: the Argument Interchange Format (AIF) [RAH 09], which has not primarily been developed for argument mining purposes but which may suit the task as well as different lines of research (see also section 6.2.3). Moreover, as M. Lippi and P. Torroni [LIP 16] emphasize it, the development of Internet and the myriad of arguments expressed online provide an unprecedented venue for argument mining but, up to now, argument mining systems have only been tested on relatively small corpora, which raises the question of scalability. Finally, most of the argument mining efforts have been applied to English, but they are easily portable to other languages or domains, by annotating corpora in those other languages (see also section 6.5.9).

It must be noted as well that systems that rely upon a pipeline approach (such as [SAI 12] or [STA 17]) present another challenge since potential errors arising during the first steps of the pipeline influence the results of the following steps. For instance, if a unit has been wrongly annotated as a claim in the first stages, the resulting argument structure detection will be false.

7.5. Conclusion

We have seen that argument mining highly mirrors argument annotation: manual annotations can serve to train, test and develop systems that will automatically replicate the tasks. Such systems find applications in various domains such as the medical and legal fields or public deliberation.

While we have seen in Chapter 6 that manual analyses of argument are highly challenging, we can see that automatic analysis is even more complex, yielding disparate and lower results. Nevertheless, the literature review presented in section 7.3 clearly shows that argument mining is still in its early stages without widely accepted and established annotation schemes, approaches and evaluation. We believe, however, that the systems proposed so far will allow argument mining techniques to evolve and improve. Argument mining is indeed a very recent yet extremely attractive research area; while the first works related to argument mining appeared at the beginning of 2010s (see, for instance, [MOC 09, MOC 11, SAI 12]), a large number of conferences and events dedicated to argument mining has started to attract scholars: the first ACL workshop on argument mining took place in 2014 and international conferences such as COMMA have since received many papers related to this topic.

The aim of this chapter was to provide an overview of the goals, applications and techniques for argument mining. The following chapter, instead, can serve as a concrete – yet brief – example of the argument mining task.

8

A Computational Model and a Simple Grammar-Based Implementation

The theoretical aspects of argumentation have been developed in Chapters 1 and 2. The linguistic dimensions of argumentation are presented in Chapters 3 and 4, where some of the main linguistic features of the structure of claims and justifications have been presented. Then, how the various parts of arguments can be annotated is discussed in Chapter 6. The main systems and technical challenges have been presented in Chapter 7.

Given these elements, this chapter introduces a way to model these observations in a computational way together with implementation elements, so that arguments can be mined in various types of texts. The approach presented here is based on grammars, a universal model that can be implemented in various ways. We show, in particular, how systematic observations of arguments and their annotations can progressively be modeled by means of grammars. The implementation presented here is simple: our goal is to show a possible implementation of the linguistic principles developed in the previous chapters and how the data identified via annotation as typical argumentation can be used.

This chapter deals first with the identification of argumentative units, which is a very difficult problem, but a preliminary step toward the other processes. Then, lexical and grammatical formalisms and data used in structure analysis are developed so that the reader may see what features are necessary and how they can be handled. Then, sample patterns to identify claims, and then supports and attacks are presented. This chapter concludes by an analysis of strength.

The examples are made as readable as possible. Their main motivation is to introduce a method that must be enhanced by the practitioner depending on his/her argument mining context and the expected accuracy of the results. The programming examples are given in logic programming, they are simple and readable. These examples can be implemented in a diversity of programming languages, in particular via scripts or rewrite rules. Learning procedures require different technologies, they are in general based on large volumes of annotated data. Finally, hybrid systems make a joint use of linguistic considerations and data acquired via learning.

8.1. Identification of argumentative units

Identifying arguments and their various parts or components is a difficult task. Given a text, the first challenge is to identify text spans that are argumentative. This means segmenting a text into small units and precisely identifying where argumentative units start and where they end. While some may overlap, let us consider that each unit is distinct from the others. The challenge is in fact twofold: identifying that a text fragment is argumentative and defining its boundaries. This section develops methodological elements and then grammatical criteria to identify these units in a number of linguistics situations.

8.1.1. *Challenges raised by the identification of argumentative units*

A unit boundaries are characterized by a beginning and an ending. Identifying these correspond to two different problems that require different linguistic analyses. These units, which are text segments, are frequently called argumentative discourse units (ADUs) compared with elementary discourse units (EDUs), which are used in discourse to characterize elementary discourse units. This is developed in depth in [PEL 13]. However, as shall be seen below, ADUs and EDUs are substantially different.

The notion of ADU is rather fuzzy, with different possible levels of granularity. ADUs can be elementary structures such as claims, justifications (supports) or attacks. They can also be a combination of several of these elements when they are adjacent, which is not necessarily the case. The content of these ADUs is somewhat fuzzy. Our observations show that arguments and argument components are often complex hierarchical structures where there is a main element, for example a claim or an attack, and peripheral elements such as secondary claims, bound to the main one, or discourse structures that add useful information such as restrictions or illustrations to the main structure. These secondary or peripheral elements cannot be separated from the main ones, unless a specific notation is used to indicate that they are related.

ADUs are difficult to identify and subject to disagreement among annotators (see Chapter 6). Since this is the first step of an argument mining system, whatever its architecture (e.g. pipeline), it is crucial to have decision criteria that are simple, reusable and as close as possible to the observations. In addition to Chapter 5, examples of annotated ADUs can be found at http://argumentationmining. disi.unibo.it/ resources.html.

This section presents some elements to identify argumentative units. First, observations are presented and then a modeling method is introduced. While there are some stable elements that can be used to delimit these units, there are also many ad hoc cues that depend on the topic, the media and the type of exchange, such as dialog, blog and news article. Therefore, this section develops an analysis method, not a comprehensive system. While ADUs endings are frequently characterized by the end of a sentence, connectors or conjunctions, the beginning of an ADU may be the beginning of a sentence. However, it is frequently necessary to skip the first words of a sentence, which do not really have any argumentative content but are rather introductory structures. To give a flavor of this latter case, here are a few real-life examples where the argumentative content starts after some words are skipped; these are noted in parenthesis:

> *(For me,) women safety is actually a very significant challenge.*
> *(In that case,) I would refute the notion that these people were terrorists, they just struggle for their lives.*
> *(This would lead me to say that) not all debt is bad.*
> *(The problem is that, at the moment,) inflation is so high that consumers have difficulties asking for loans.*
> *(We have to realize that) debt is necessary and useful for the economy.*

Identifying the elements to skip at the beginning of a sentence is quite tricky, even for annotators. A strategy, developed below is to specify what elements could start *a priori* an argumentative statement instead of specifying those that must be skipped. These units should also be kept minimal, skipping unnecessary comments.

Beside the main criteria presented above used to segment texts to identify ADUs, the feasibility of using crowd-sourcing and novice annotators to identify finer details and nuances of the basic argumentative units focusing on limited context is developed in [GHO 13]. R. Artstein and M. Poesio [ART 08] develop methods to measure the interannotator agreement on ADU analysis. Finally, E. Cabrio and S. Villata [CAB 13] propose an original approach to argument mining including ADU identification based on textual entailment, which is a promising technique, but quite difficult to develop.

8.1.2. *Some linguistic techniques to identify ADUs*

ADUs can be identified using two different, if not opposite, techniques: an analysis based on grammatical cues and the use of machine learning. Machine learning techniques are frequently used because they are based on annotated texts, therefore accuracy and precision should be relatively good with respect to the domain and style being considered. However, it seems that machine learning for argument mining is difficult to develop for two main reasons: (1) a very large annotated corpus is necessary to categorize boundaries and (2) the diversity of expressions may be so large that ambiguities and errors are possible and difficult to identify. A grammar-based approach is also difficult to carry out. Developing grammars, based on annotated corpus observations, requires some categorization and generalization efforts from human programmers. However, this approach can be developed gradually with valuable results at each stage. Since this book deals with the linguistic aspects of argument mining, this latter approach is favored below.

The simple principles and rules presented in this section show how ADUs can be identified and segmented. These rules are designed to be illustrations, which must not hide the complexity of the task that is entailed by the large diversity of syntactic constructions and lexical items found in corpora. Several examples given below illustrate the language complexity of argumentative texts.

8.1.2.1. *The sentence level*

An argumentative unit is basically a simple sentence composed of a main proposition S, with a main verb. Noun phrases (NPs) may be associated with relative clauses. The main verb may be modified by a modal or a negation. The proposition S can be introduced by a propositional attitude verb or may be associated with one or more discourse structures. In that case, the unit starts at the beginning of the sentence and ends at the punctuation mark (usually a full stop, an interrogative or an exclamation mark).

This informal description can be roughly modeled by the following rule, for English:

ADU → {introductory term}, {discourse structure*}, {Verb(propatt)}, S, {discourse structure*}.
S → NP(subject), {modal}, {negation}, Verb(main), {NP(object)}, {PP}.
NP → determiner, noun, {relative-clause}.

{ } encodes the optional character of symbols, while the "*" encodes the fact that this symbol may be repeated a finite number of times. Modals include a number of higher-order verbs that modify the verb and have scope over the whole proposition. Verbs may be inflected, possibly in association with auxiliaries.

This being said, ADUs may be difficult to identify precisely because of the diversity of expressions they contain and the indirect style that is frequently used. Let us consider two examples taken from real texts:

I think we need to go further together a bit more.

In this example, *I think* is a propositional attitude construction that has a sentential complement, which is the main statement S. S contains a specific modal expression *we need*. It has no adjoined discourse structures. The next example:

> *What we are financing is the ability of people to smooth out the peaks and troughs of their income and expenditure, for example around Boxing Day.*

includes an introductory construction *What* followed by a complex statement formulated in an indirect way. This example ends by a discourse structure of type illustration:

> *for example around Boxing Day.*

It is difficult to precisely identify where the ADU starts: from *we are* or from *ability*? It is obviously crucial to have in the ADU the elements that can be debated. Probably, in this example, the term *financing* is the debatable term.

Statements that include connectors binding two basic sentences originate with two ADUs (see section 6.1.1), as in:

> *Their monthly incomes vary enormously, but their core bills don't.*

with:

> ADU1 = *Their monthly incomes vary enormously,* and
> ADU2 = *their core bills don't,*

the connector *but* does not belong to any of the ADUs; it simply connects them and provides some orientation elements. In a number of cases, some contextual elements in ADU1 must be included into ADU2 to guarantee its conceptual independence.

The same observation holds for conjunctions such as *and* when they bind two propositions. This situation is more difficult to process as the scope of a conjunction may be ambiguous, a well-known problem in language processing. In a number of cases, this conjunction is simply realized by the comma. Complex sentences can be decomposed into *a priori* any finite number of ADUs as expressed in the following simple rules:

> S → ADU, (connector, ADU)*.
> S → ADU, (conjunction, ADU)*.

8.1.2.2. *Interrogative forms*

ADUs can be formulated as interrogative forms. This is, for example, the case when someone challenges someone else on a debatable topic. This is also relatively frequent for claims that, for example, open a debate. Interrogative forms may include very diverse structures, among which are adverbs or adjectives (e.g. *is it reasonable to...*). It is therefore not straightforward to identify where an ADU starts, since the interrogative words are in general not part of it. Modals are frequent, they are used to express doubts or to raise a question with some care (e.g. *what would be ...*).

ADUs can also be rhetorical questions, frequently introduced by cues such as *why should* and *should it be*. Although rhetorical questions are not meant to stimulate debates since the response is implicit or formulated by the same utterer, they are nevertheless argumentative units and can open a debate if the utterer's response is not satisfactory or subject to controversies. Rhetorical questions may also convey doxa: opinions which are supposed to be shared by a large majority of people in a group. These commonly admitted opinions can however be discussed or refined, in particular at specific occasions.

ADUs formulated as interrogative forms suggest debates in a more direct way than affirmative questions since they clearly open a discussion:

> *What would be the advantage to have a high level of debts for a standard citizen?.*

They appear more frequently in debates or on informal supports such as blogs. They are less frequent in written texts, but may be used as titles to open more efficiently a debate. There are many ways to formulate a question, however, looking at corpora, the most frequent linguistic cues include, for example, *are we supposed to, do you think/believe/assume, is it the case that, why is that, what would* and *where does*. Interrogative structures can roughly be modeled by a rule such as:

> ADU → {interrogative form}, {Verb(propatt)}, S, {discourse structure*}, "?".

There are obviously a number of variants of this typical rule.

8.1.2.3. *Conditionals*

Conditional expressions may also introduce ADUs. They are relatively close to questions. They add a context to the ADU, which is formulated in the condition:

> *If we assume that Ebola is a dangerous disease, infected areas should develop large vaccination campaigns as soon as possible.*
> *Assuming that Ebola is growing rapidly, research efforts must be funded rapidly.*

The context as well as the ADU can be debated. Conditionals can be represented as propositions. However, conditions are rather treated as discourse structures that introduce, for example, restrictions.

The structure of ADUs introduced by a condition is typically:

> ADU → {conditional phrase}, {discourse structure*}, S, {discourse structure*}.

A conditional phrase is a proposition that is preceded by a term such as *if* or an expression that induces a hypothesis such as *assuming that*.

8.1.2.4. *Meta-discourse articulations*

Meta-discourse articulations include a large variety of expressions that are used to introduce argumentative structures or to clearly indicate how they are related. These articulations are used in almost every type of argumentative discourse to organize a discourse, to structure arguments, to introduce them or to produce conclusions, just to cite the main uses [SCH 80, ADE 10]. In debates, moderators make extensive use of meta-discourse articulations to control the directions taken by each speaker and to come back to the main topics being debated. These articulations contribute to the clarity of argumentation by making links between units more explicit and less ambiguous than when they remain implicit or when punctuation is used.

In Chapter 2, section 2.2.3, we show different organizations for arguments, in particular for attacks and supports: multiple premises, coordinative premises and subordinative premises. Each of these categories has its internal organizational logic and is associated with specific meta-discourse articulations and possibly intonation in oral argumentation.

These articulations are not parts of ADUs, nor are they parts of an argumentation network, however their role is important to understand an argumentation. Some of these forms are close to interrogative forms, while others stimulate exchanges. These articulations include terms or expressions, among many others, where P and S are propositions:

> *the question is P,*
> *let us now ask Mr/Mrs M his position,*
> *You had a different view on this point did you?,*
> *an opposite view would be,*
> *a counterargument can be developed around,*
> *other participants think the opposite or differently:*
> *isn't it the case that P,*
> *the problem is that P,*
> *Let us consider the next question,*
> *S are very important/specific problems,*
> *a very specific case is.*

8.2. Mining for claims

Let us consider a situation where a text may contain one or more claims. These claims may be related or independent. Let us assume that ADUs are either identified prior to any analysis of argument components or identified in conjunction with an analysis of their argumentative content. This is essentially an architecture and a strategy problem, which however may have consequences on the system efficiency. Each task can indeed be characterized independently. Let us first characterize the formalisms and the resources that are used and then present claim analysis patterns.

8.2.1. *The grammar formalisms*

The main linguistic features typical of claims are presented in Chapter 3, section 3.1. The reader may note the large diversity of factors that may contribute to the characterization of a claim. Let us show in this section how these can be modeled and implemented. For that purpose, two simple formalisms are used in this presentation: grammars or patterns. To improve readability, grammars are used in this book to account for local constructions where they contribute to developing linguistic generalizations, whereas patterns are used to characterize high-level structures such as claims. Patterns could easily be implemented as grammars. Grammars as well as patterns can easily be implemented in a number of programming languages or environments. For example, the different types of unification grammars developed in the literature from the past two decades can be used.

In this book, the use of Prolog and Definite Clause Grammars (DCGs) [PER 80] is used to encode grammars, while Dislog, an extension to Prolog to process discourse structures, is used in a simplified way to describe and implement patterns. DCGs have the form of rewrite rules where grammar symbols may include arguments to encode various features or to elaborate results (e.g. [SEL 85, SHI 86]). In [PER 80], DCGs are compared to augmented transition networks (ATNs), which is a more procedural way to process language. More details and an implementation of Dislog can be found in TextCoop [SAI 12]. The presentation provided here should however be sufficiently simple to be accessible to any reader familiar with the notion of templates and rewrite rules.

DCGs are context-free grammars where symbols are augmented with attributes. Controls on the content of these attributes can be implemented by means of Prolog clauses. This is a very simple and ready-to-use formalism. The role of these attributes, expressed by means of logical variables, is to allow controls such as morphological agreement and to construct representations such as syntactic trees or semantic representations. For example,

```
NP(N) --> det(N), noun(N).
```

It says that an NP is composed of a determiner followed by a noun, the variable N, repeated in each symbol "det" and "noun", represents here the feature "number". Its co-occurrence in each symbol imposes that the determiner and the noun have the same number when it is morphologically marked, in other terms they must agree in number. The NP symbol also includes this variable to indicate that the NP inherits of the number of the noun. The noun is called in linguistics the head of the construction of the NP. This type of agreement is more crucial for Romance languages, for example, where the gender is also marked, than it is for English.

Lexical items are represented in a similar fashion:

```
noun(sing) --> [car].
noun(plu) --> [computers].
det(sing) --> [the].
det(plu) --> [most].
```

In this simple example, the determiner is singular and has no gender. The symbols "sing" and "plu" are defined *a priori* by the programmer and must be used consistently throughout the whole grammar and lexicon. This representation says that the symbol noun is a preterminal that derives in car or computers.

DCGs also allow the specification of more complex constraints such as semantic agreement, for example between a verb and its subject and complements. It also allows the specification of syntactic constraints such as subcategorization frames.

Patterns are declarative structures, i.e. the way they are processed is not specified at this level. This is also the case for DCGs, although they are presented as a rewriting process. In our case, patterns are close to regular expressions, where symbols may also include features expressed by means of logical variables. For example, assuming that a claim is characterized by the presence of an evaluative expression, then a pattern such as

```
Claim :  [BOS, gap(X), Evaluative(Type, Orient, Strength),
          gap(Y), EOS]
```

allows the recognition of such claims. Briefly, in this pattern:

1) *BOS* represents the beginning of a sentence, it is an abstract notion with no linguistic realization beside the presence of a capital letter on the first word of a sentence;

2) *EOS* represents the end of a sentence, in general it is a punctuation mark such as a full stop, an interrogative or exclamation mark;

3) the *gap* symbols stand for finite, possibly empty, sequences of words of no present interest;

4) *Evaluative* is a grammar symbol describing the structure of an evaluative expression. The evaluative expression has, *a priori*, a *type*, an *orientation* and a *strength*. This is discussed below.

For example, in:

Vaccination against Ebola is necessary.

– BOS starts at "Vaccination", but does not include this word;

– gap(X) skips "Vaccination against Ebola";

– Evaluative = "is necessary";

– gap(Y) is empty;

– EOS is the full stop.

The fact that the evaluative expression includes the auxiliary can be debated. It is included here because such an expression may include modals such as "could be" instead of just "is". This would allow to take into account the impact of *could* in the evaluation of the strength of the claim.

8.2.2. *Lexical issues*

Let us now elaborate a few typical rules for the Evaluative symbol introduced above following the features given in section 3.1. The first structure that needs to be developed is a lexicon that includes for each lexical category, besides lexical and syntactic features of interest for a parser, some form of semantic typing that would allow to evaluate a potential polarity and a strength for the whole claim.

Lexical entries are represented by means of predicate-argument structures as shown above. The term "argument" must not be confused with the notion of argument in argumentation. Predicates are composed of a functor (its name) and arguments. An argument is simply a fixed position with a precise role and content. The categorizations and the examples given below are standard representations, they can however be adapted or revised depending on the argument mining approach and the needs in terms of lexical content and control.

For adjectives such as *easy, difficult, toxic, efficient* and *unsafe*, lexical entries such as the following can be defined:

```
adjective(manner, positive, average) --> [easy].
adjective(manner, negative, average) --> [difficult].
adjective(state, negative, high) --> [toxic].
adjective(process, positive, average) --> [efficient].
adjective(process, negative, high) --> [unsafe].
```

where the element to the right of the arrow is the word to be derived from the preterminal symbol "adjective". The word is represented as a list to manage cases where it is composed of several elements (e.g. [dark, blue]).

In the predicate "adjective", the first argument is a form of semantic typing for the adjective: the kind of property it refers to or modifies in a noun. In our example, terms such as "manner", "state" or "process" are used: these are arbitrary for the purpose of illustration and other tags can be preferred. It is, however, recommended to use standard linguistic classifications that are commonly admitted and reusable. The second argument indicates the polarity, positive or negative and, finally, the last argument indicates the *a priori* strength: low, average or high. Any other scale can be used, for example, with five positions as usually used in theoretical argumentation, but with no real justification. Note that the polarity of a few adjectives may change over domains. This is in particular the case for higher-order adjectives: while *a light meal* has an ambiguous polarity depending on the eater's needs, *a high salary* is positive whereas *a high taxation level* is negative for the citizen.

Verbs with a positive or negative polarity are described in a similar manner. If we omit the subcategorization frame and the morphological aspects, of little interest for the present purpose, we have the following examples, where the first argument of "verb" encodes the orientation and the second the strength:

```
verb(positive, average) --> [protect].
verb(positive, low) --> [prevent].
verb(negative, high) --> [destroy].
verb(negative, average) --> [damage].
```

Adverbs express different features such as necessity or possibility. They can also be intensifiers or have a temporal dimension that can be debated. The combination constraints of adverbs with verbs or with adjectives is quite complex. However, this information is not crucial for our purpose, it is therefore not specified here. Of interest are their polarity when it exists and their strength:

```
adverb(intensifier, _ , low) --> [possibly].
adverb(necessity, _ , high) --> [necessary].
adverb(intensifier, _ , average) --> [very].
```

Features that are not relevant or that cannot be specified at this stage are represented by the empty variable denoted as "_". In terms of strength, "very" adds a level of intensity to the adjective it modifies, as described in section 3.3.1. Adverbials are represented in a similar way, where the word structure is a list of several terms (e.g. [most, definitely]). These adverbials of opinion expression develop doubts or questions around a fact, making it debatable:

Vaccination against Ebola is most definitely necessary.

Lexical resources are represented as follows:

```
adverb(opinion, _ , strong) --> [most, definitely].
adverb(opinion, _ , weak) --> [is, usually].
adverb(opinion, _ , average) --> [surely].
adverb(opinion, _ , weak) --> [probably].
```

Adverbs as well as verbs or adjectives can be classified in more than one category. Modals are represented in a similar way. They modify the strength of a statement. This is encoded by a simple argument with three possible values: weaken, neutral, reinforce, as in:

```
adverb(modal, _, weaken) --> [could].
adverb(modal, _, reinforce) --> [must].
adverb(modal, _, reinforce) --> [should].
adverb(modal, _, reinforce) --> [have, to].
adverb(modal, _, reinforce) --> [has, to].
```

Modals are generic, and they are not, therefore, associated with any semantic typing. The way they are associated with other lexical terms is described by a grammar and possible restrictions.

Claims can be expressed in the interrogative form, as described above. Similarly to modals, a strength can be added in particular for complex interrogative forms that contain modals or adverbials. A type "rhetorical" could be added for interrogative forms starting by *why should P?*. A simple representation for interrogative form lexical entries is the following:

```
pronoun(interrogative, neutral, average) --> [what, would, be].
pronoun(interrogative, neutral, average) -->
        [is, it, the, case, that].
pronoun(interrogative, rhetorical, average) --> [why, should].
pronoun(interrogative, neutral, strong) -->
        [is, it, necessarily, the, case, that].
```

The lexical entries given above are simple illustrations. These lexical entries risk being very numerous, it is therefore advised to adapt these entries and generalize them via a local grammar that would categorize the different terms found in these entries such as modals, adjectives or auxiliaries.

Finally, verbs of propositional attitude are associated with a semantic type, in particular belief, psychological, performative, report and epistemic. These verbs belong to the class of control verbs that subcategorize for a sentential complement, which is the argument. This is not developed here since this is a syntax problem largely developed in various grammar formalisms such as Head-Driven Phrase Structure Grammars (HPSGs) and Lexical Functional Grammars (LFGs); these are briefly presented in [SEL 85]. Due to its specific syntax, a feature "propatt" (for *propositional attitude*) is included in the lexical representation to indicate the verb category. This feature is a kind of semantic type used to filter out incorrect constructions. Other high-level verb categories could be "state", "modal", "epistemic" and "action". Finally, a strength factor is added in the third argument. Verbs are represented as follows:

```
verb(propatt, psychological, average) --> [feel].
verb(propatt, report, strong) --> [claim].
verb(propatt, report, average) --> [report].
verb(propatt, epistemic, average) --> [think].
verb(propatt, epistemic, strong) --> [am, convinced].
verb(propatt, psychological, low) --> [imagine].
```

Some form of strength could possibly be added to these representations on the basis of a very refined analysis of strength. These verbs may also include verb compounds and verb particle constructions such as: [worried, about], [intrigued, by], in that case some morphology is added on the verb, as for the "convinced" example above.

8.2.3. *Grammatical issues*

Let us now show how grammatical constructions, in general related to local phenomena such the Evaluative symbol given above, can be implemented by means of grammars. The format given here is generic and can be quite directly reformulated into a variety of grammatical formalisms or templates, depending on the linguistic approach adopted in the argument mining system that is considered.

A first example is the modification of an adjective by an adverb, which, in general, reinforces or weakens its strength, as described in section 3.3.1. It is written as follows in DCG format:

```
adj(SemType, Orientation, Strength) -->
    adverb(intensifier, _, St1),
    adjective(SemType, Orientation, St2),
    {combine(Strength, St1, St2)}.
```

This example reads as follows: an "adj" phrase (adjective phrase, AP) is composed of an adverb followed by an adjective. The adverb must be of semantic type (SemType) "intensifier", and it induces a certain strength St1. The adjective has any SemType:

manner, state or process; it has a certain Orientation and an intrinsic strength St2. The "adj" phrase inherits the orientation and the semantic type of the adjective. The Strength variable encodes the strength of the "adj" phrase, which is a combination of St1 and St2. The elaboration of the strength of an expression is provided below. Note that if the adverb is a compound form such as *most definitely*, a strength that includes all the words must be defined.

Then, the symbol Evaluative can be defined, among many other possibilities, as follows:

```
Evaluative(SemType, Orientation, Strength) -->
    aux(be,St1),
    adj(SemType, Orientation, St2),
    {combine(Strength, St1, St2)}.
aux(be, neutral) --> auxiliary(be).
aux(be, Strength) -->
    modal(Strength),
    auxiliary(be).
aux(be, Strength) -->
    modal(St1),
    adverb(modal, _, St2),
    {combine(Strength, St1, St2)}.
    auxiliary(be).
adverb(modal, _, weaken) --> [could].
auxiliary(be) --> [is].
auxiliary(be) --> [are].
auxiliary(be) --> [was].
```

The strength induced by the auxiliary when it is composed of a modal is combined with the strength of the "adj" phrase to produce the global strength of the evaluative expression. According to this example, the modal *could* weakens the adjective phrase by the uncertainty it introduces while *must* reinforces it.

The case of negation is interesting since in general it reverses the strength and the orientation (also called the polarity) of the statement, as in:

Vaccination against Ebola is not necessary.

where the expression *not necessary* is approximately equivalent to *unnecessary*. The rule for an Evaluative that includes a negation is written as follows:

```
Evaluative(SemType, Orientation, Strength) -->
    aux(be,St1),
    negation,
    adj(SemType, Orient, St2),
```

```
{combine(Strength, St1, St2),
 reverseStrength(St3, Strength)
 reverseOrient(Orientation, Orient)}.
negation --> [not].
negation --> [does, not].
negation --> [do, not].
negation --> [will, not].
aux(be, neutral) --> auxiliary(be).
aux(be, Strength) -->
   modal(Strength),
   auxiliary(be).
```

The predicate `reverseStrength` unifies `Strength` with the opposite value of St3. For example, in a system with three values, "strong" becomes "weak". Similarly, the predicate `reverseOrient` reverses the orientation: "attack" becomes "support" and vice versa. Note that negation may not be so radical, as for example in *may not* where there is both an effect on the orientation and on the strength, which is weakened.

As explained above, an evaluative expression can be a verb such as *protect, prevent, destroy, damage* or any combination of one these verbs possibly with an appropriate modal, as in: *could damage* or any combination with a negation. The corresponding rules are written as follows:

```
Evaluative(SemType, Orientation, Strength) -->
   modal(St1),            % Modal + verb
   verb(SemType, Orient, St2),
   {combine(Strength, St1, St2)}.
Evaluative(SemType, Orientation, Strength) -->
   modal(St1),            % Modal + negation + verb
   negation,
   verb(SemType, Orient, St2),
   {combine(Strength, St1, St2),
    reverseOrient(Orientation, Orient)}.
Evaluative(SemType, Orientation, Strength) -->
   negation,       % negation + verb
   verb(SemType, Orient, Strength),
   {reverseOrient(Orientation, Orient)}.
Evaluative(SemType, Orientation, Strength) -->
   verb(SemType, Orientation, Strength).   % verb alone
```

The above examples of evaluative constructions remain simple and can be more complex in real situations. However, the principles remain the same and more rules of this form can be developed.

8.2.4. *Templates for claim analysis*

Given the formalisms described above, and lexical and grammatical resources, let us now show how claims can be identified from elementary text units, as defined in the first section of this chapter. A claim is characterized by the presence of an evaluative expression in the text unit that is considered. A pattern such as:

```
Claim : [BOS, gap(X), Evaluative(Type, Orient, St2), gap(Y), EOS]
```

defines the essence of the structure of a claim. It is a sentence in which the evaluative expression has a Type, inherited from the elements it is composed of, an Orientation and a Strength, also determined from each component of the evaluative expression. A claim can also include a propositional attitude construction which, in general, appears to the left of the claim:

I strongly believe that vaccination against Ebola is necessary.

Such a construction is processed by the following template:

```
Claim : [BOS, gap(X), VerbProp(propatt, TypeVerb, St1),
         gap(Y), Evaluative(Type, Orient, St2), gap(Z), EOS]
```

where gap(X) skips, for example, any subject or introductory expression. Then the pattern indicates that a propositional attitude verb must be found, followed by another gap before the evaluative expression is found. The propositional attitude verb structure is recognized by the following grammar:

```
VerbProp(propatt, Type, Strength) -->
    adverb(Type1, _, St1),
    verb(propatt, Type, St2),
    {combine(Strength, St1, St2)}.
VerbProp(propatt, Type, Strength) -->
    verb(propatt, Type, Strength).
```

The use of adverbs of frequency or completion in a standard statement introduces a form of doubt or uncertainty, leading to potential supports or attacks (section 3.1). This is the case for adverbs and adverbial expressions such as *frequently, almost never, seldom, systematically.* A simple pattern is then:

```
Claim: [BOS, gap(X), adverb(temporal, _, Strength), gap(Y), EOS].
adverb(temporal, _, low) --> [seldom].
adverb(temporal, _, average) --> [occasionally].
adverb(temporal, _, strong) --> [very, frequently].
```

This pattern is simple but may overrecognize structures that are not claims. It should therefore be used with caution or paired with additional controls. For example, this pattern does not say anything about the position of the adverb, nor does it impose constraints on the content of the gaps. It would be appropriate to say that these are propositions with a verb of a certain type and no negation. In Dislog, it is possible to control the type of lexical items that are skipped by a gap and to impose constraints on it. The same pattern can be written for adverbs of completion (e.g. *not totally*) with the same remarks.

Let us now consider the introduction of discourse structures that introduce a debatable character to a statement. This is, for example, the case for illustrations, where the examples that are provided can be debated. Discourse structures are recognized by templates in Dislog. There are many ways to define an illustration. The following patterns are frequently encountered:

```
Illustration: [exp(illustration), Enumeration].
Illustration: [Enumeration, exp(illustration)].
Illustration: ['(', exp(illustration), Enumeration, ')'].
Enumeration --> NP, {',', NP}*.  % generally more complex
exp(illustration) --> [for, example].
exp(illustration) --> [as, in].
exp(illustration) --> [for, instance].
```

These patterns indicate that an illustration is introduced by a specific linguistic mark (e.g. *for example*), which is either before or after an enumeration of one or more items that constitute the illustration. An illustration may also be embedded into parentheses. A pattern where an illustration is adjoined to a sentence S and then to a claim is represented as follows:

```
Discourse structure: [BOS, S, Illustration, gap(Y), EOS].
Claim: [BOS, Claim, gap(X), Illustration, gap(Y), EOS].
```

In most cases, the gap(Y) is empty since the illustration ends the sentence, unless other discourse structures appear after the illustration.

Finally, claims can have interrogative forms, either as simple questions or as rhetorical questions. A simple pattern is:

```
Claim: [BOS, gap(X), pronoun(interrogative, Type1, St1),
        gap(Y), Evaluative(Type, Orient, St2), gap(Z), EOS].
```

Then the strength of the claim is a composition of the two strengths St1 and St2. The orientation is *a priori* not affected by the interrogative forms, although negation could play a role.

8.3. Mining for supports and attacks

The main linguistic characteristics of supports and attacks are defined in section 3.2. An important challenge, when identifying argumentative relations, is the problem of relatedness between a claim and a support or an attack, i.e. how to make sure that a statement is indeed thematically related to a claim and that it plays the role of a support or an attack. This problem is crucial when claims and supports or attacks are not adjacent in a text, possibly not in the same document. We will not develop the problem of relatedness in this section, since it involves knowledge and inferencing. The linguistic and conceptual aspects of this problem are developed in section 4.2. Let us concentrate on the recognition of isolated supports or attacks and pairs claim – support or attack when they are adjacent or close in an argumentative text, where the reference problems raised by relatedness are not crucial.

8.3.1. *Structures introduced by connectors*

Supports or attacks are in general linked to a claim by means of a connector when they appear in the same sentence. As explained in section 2.1, the claim is the conclusion and the support is the premise. The standard form is "premise because conclusion" or "support $\Rightarrow$ claim". Supports or attacks and claims are linked by means of various types of connectors. It is also possible to have two adjacent sentences that develop each structure claim, support/attack. Connectors are quite different in this second situation (e.g. *the reason is that, let me explain, let me motivate*) or may not exist: the fact that the sentences are adjacent could suggest a causal relation between them, which is inferred by the reader. Finally, when a claim and its supports or attacks are not adjacent, then a short introductory phrase may indicate the link, for example, *concerning "claim topic", reasons are....*

In the case of unit adjacency in a single sentence, several types of connectors are used, these have an influence on the nature of the claim – support/attack. These connectors also have a large diversity of lexical structure: they may be simple connectors or they may be verbal forms or compounds. Let us mention the main ones here with an associated semantic type:

```
connector(causal) --> [because].
connector(causal) --> [since].
connector(causal) --> [due, to].
connector(purpose) --> [in, order, to].
connector(purpose) --> [to, avoid].
connector(purpose) --> [to, prevent].
connector(result) --> [therefore].
connector(concessive) --> [although].
connector(concessive) --> [nonetheless].
```

```
connector(contrast) --> [whereas].
connector(contrast) --> [but].
```

A support or an attack is then a statement S introduced by one of the above connectors:

```
Support, Attack: [connector(Type), S, EOS],
  member-of(Type, [causal, purpose, result, concessive, contrast]).
```

This rule makes a control on the nature of the type of the connector to filter out relations that are not argumentative (e.g. temporal). This is realized by means of the predefined predicate member-of(X, S), which is true if X is a member of the set S. The taking into account of the semantic type of the connector is crucial to determine the nature and the strength of the link between a claim and a support or an attack. Besides the connector that is used, attacks or supports are determined on the basis of their content in order to identify their orientation and strength.

8.3.2. *Structures introduced by propositional attitudes*

In some cases, supports or attacks are defined on the basis of a specific propositional attitude verb, which is used in conjunction with – or instead of – the connector. This is, for example, the case in dialogs with the use of propositional attitude verbs and verb particle constructions (typically verbs associated with a preposition: *switch off, boil down*). To implement these structures, a subtype of the type "propatt" defined above can be introduced:

```
verb(propatt(support), epistemic, average) --> [agree, with].
verb(propatt(attack), epistemic, strong) --> [reject].
verb(propatt(attack), epistemic, average) --> [disagree, with].
```

Such statements are in general expressed in independent sentences that are adjacent or close to the claim in a text or a dialog. A simple pattern that accounts for this phenomenon is:

```
Support: [BOS, gap(X), verb(propatt(support), Type, Strength),
             S, EOS].
```

where gap(X) skips in particular subjects and adverbs.

8.3.3. *Other linguistic forms to express supports or attacks*

There are other ways based on linguistic cues to support or attack a claim, besides the use of connectors. Let us illustrate these alternatives here. However, a number of cases where there are no explicit connectors require knowledge and inferencing.

Besides the standard "yes", agreement can be expressed by approval expressions such as *most definitely, indeed*. These expressions are very numerous, in particular in spoken language. Agreement can also be expressed by just repeating or paraphrasing the claim, possibly adding a few details or some elaborations:

> *Vaccination must be developed in Ebola-infected areas,*
> *vaccination is necessary,*
> *vaccination should be extended to larger perimeters around infected areas.*

The initial claim is reinforced by additional information, the last two utterances are therefore supports of the claim. The adjunction of the pronoun *yes* would obviously contribute to this support.

A simple and direct way to express a disagreement, and therefore an attack, is the use of negation. Given a claim C, uttering not(C) is a form of attack:

> *vaccine against Ebola is necessary.*
> *No, vaccine against Ebola is not necessary at all.*
> *I think that the vaccine against Ebola is not necessary/unnecessary.*

This form of attack is however quite limited because it does not contain any form of justification. Note the different ways to express negation besides using the adverb "no".

Next, given a claim, using positive terms in a dialog would indicate a support, while negative terms would induce an attack, even without any justification:

> *Lowering taxes is good for the population,*
> *I have some sympathy for this decision,*
> *I am afraid this decision will have negative consequences for the state budget, I am surprised by this decision.*

The term *sympathy* is positive and indicates a support to the claim, while *I am afraid, am surprised* induce attacks. Terms such as *recognize, accept* and *share* go in the same direction than the claim. They are forms of acceptance. Terms such as *surprised, uncomfortable with, suspect* indicate, with various strengths or nuances, that they are attacks. The role of *negative consequences* in general is difficult: it may depend on the nature of the consequences.

The use of opposite terms in a claim and an utterance suggests an attack. This mainly concerns adjectives but also nouns that can be classified according to the principles of antonym construction:

the government must be on the side of the nationalists,
the government is on the side of the imperialists.

Temporally oriented linguistic cues mays also be used: *right time* versus *too early* these allow the induction of supports and attacks. However, some of these terms are subject to contextual interpretation, for example *frequently* may be interpreted in either a positive or negative way depending on what this adverb applies to. We reach here the limits of the contribution of linguistic cues to determine orientation.

From an analysis point of view, these terms can be recognized in a way similar to connectors, they may however not appear at the beginning of a sentence:

```
Support: [BOS, gap(X), positionexp(Orientation, Type, Strength),
    {S}, EOS].
positionexp(positive, _, moderate) --> [have, sympathy, for].
positionexp(positive, _, average) --> [yes].
positionexp(negative, _, average) --> [afraid, of].
```

The symbol `positionexp` describes an expression of position as illustrated above. Note that the justification S is optional.

8.4. Evaluating strength

Strength is essentially, in our view, a linguistic dimension that takes into account the individual strengths of the words that compose a claim, a support or an attack. Strength is a certain composition, possibly weighted, of these individual strengths. Persuasion is somewhat different: if it relies on strength evaluation, it also takes into account a number of contextual factors that go beyond a linguistic model. For example, in a debate with strong controversies, a claim will be judged "average" even if it contains strong terms, whereas in a polite and smooth debate, the same claim will be judged "strong" because it contrasts with the other claims, supports or attacks.

Evaluating strength is difficult. Let us show here a way to implement it, using a five value scale, inherited from the lexical items scale:

```
(very weak, weak, average, strong, very strong).
```

Discrete values are relatively easy to integrate in a strength metrics. Using a continuous scale is much more difficult and also raises the validity of the lexical description of strength. Strength evaluation is crucial in argumentation to elaborate conclusions from an argumentation graph by sorting attacks and supports and, recursively, attacks or supports of attacks, etc. Strength evaluation will always remain an approximation.

Let us propose in this section a simple model which (1) can be sufficient in a number of cases and (2) which can be extended in several directions depending on what needs to be modeled. In the examples above, strength is basically implemented via the predefined predicate:

```
combine(Strength, St1, St2).
```

In the model below, we assume that the contribution to strength of each linguistic element has the same weight. Other weighting systems could be developed where the weight of verb would be higher than the weight of an adverb with which it is combined. Besides the fact that this view is somewhat arbitrary, introducing refined weights would entail to develop scale that could be continuous and no longer discrete. In the lexical entries developed below, we have postulated three strength values. With the possibility to weaken or reinforce one of these values, we need to have, in the end, a five-value system. This five-value system is frequently used in theoretical argumentation.

The definition of the combine predicate is based on the set of all strength combinations that may occur. Since the predicate deals with pairs of strengths to determine a resulting strength, the complexity is not too high and the conceptual validity remains acceptable. This predicate is then defined as follows, note that other combinations could be foreseen:

```
combine(very_weak, weak, weak). % weak  +  weak is very_weak
combine(weak, average, weak).
combine(average, weak, strong).
combine(very_strong, strong, strong).
combine(average, weak, strong).
combine(average, average).
```

8.5. Epilogue

In this chapter, we have developed simple implementation elements that can be reproduced and implemented in various ways. The goal was to show (1) the type of resources, in terms of lexical description and grammars, which is minimally necessary and (2) the type of processes that are needed to carry out some form of argument mining. Argument mining is still, and probably will be for a long period of time, in an emerging state. The resources that are needed and the techniques to be used are indeed very diverse and complex.

9

Non-Verbal Dimensions of Argumentation: a Challenge for Argument Mining

So far, we have concentrated on argument mining from written texts, considering the linguistic and operational dimensions of this recent research area. This is the main aim of this book. However, argumentation is an everyday life process that occurs in many situations where the textual dimension is just one dimension, probably the most important one since it conveys most of the semantic content. The non-verbal dimensions frequently play a crucial role, which may support, contradict or introduce a new perspective on the argumentation being developed. Media analysis shows that for some areas such as debates, the non-verbal aspects of argumentation may be as important as the verbal ones.

In this chapter, we show a number of non-verbal dimensions that contribute to the construction and the evaluation of an argumentation. These should be taken into account in argument mining even if they cannot in general be mined in a way similar to textual data. The sound and visual dimensions of our everyday life are considered under different angles and their contribution to argumentation is underlined and illustrated. The interactions of these non-verbal dimensions to argumentation may be quite complex and the evaluation of their impact may be quite subjective. Nevertheless, such an analysis remains crucial for a correct evaluation of an argumentation in its global context.

This chapter is an introduction to non-verbal argumentation. It is not a comprehensive synthesis and does not offer any theoretical development or any solution to this problem, which is hardly emerging.

9.1. The text and its additions

Let us first consider the dimensions that are the closest to written texts, i.e. the various pictures and icons texts may include in a number of genres.

9.1.1. *Text, pictures and icons*

Argumentation may be found in standard texts such as news, political or business analysis, dissertations or juridical deliberations and decisions. These standard texts are in general purely written texts with no non-textual additions. Documents follow well-defined structures and the language is well mastered.

Argumentation can also be found in for example, do-it-yourself documents where users are guided and warned against errors. Argumentation plays a central role in blogs and forums which are forms of written debates using a language close to the oral one. In these latter classes of documents, the purely textual part is frequently associated with pictures, diagrams or icons which complement the text or underline a certain feature. They have in general a moderate impact on the text content. Pictures and diagrams convey meaning which is often more direct to access than long and verbose texts. Icons have a more direct and simple meaning, with a widely accepted underlying meaning.

9.1.2. *Transcriptions of oral debates*

Argument mining in debates, mediation, deliberations and other oral forms of this type is in general carried out from transcripts. These transcripts are frequently poor in punctuation and in forms which are typical of oral communication such as hesitation, laugh and even repetitions, and, obviously, they do not include any form of intonation, prosody, or speed of speech. It is however of much importance to consider these dimensions since, for example:

– oral stress on a particular word or group of words indicates its importance and may change the strength of the support or attack being developed;

– taking into account intonation may indicate that a statement is a question and not an affirmation, in case there is no explicit linguistic mark such as an interrogative pronoun;

– various forms of hesitations may indicate doubt or uncertainty and can weaken the strength of the statement being developed;

– an increase in the speech speed may indicate that this is a point that needs not be discussed, which is commonly admitted, or, conversely that the utterer does not want to see debated;

– a decrease in the speech speed on a text portion may indicate either a hesitation or a form of insistence, with the focus shifted on that text portion;

– similarly, the intensity of the sound produced by the speaker, e.g. speaking louder, may indicate a form of insistence, among a few other possibilities;

– laughter and other such forms are in general quite ambiguous and depend on what is uttered and who is speaking.

These parameters could be indicated in textual transcriptions. For each of them, some precise attributes would have to be specified with a granularity that is sufficient. This will necessarily increase the text transcription workload, but the quality of the resulting analysis would be much higher [LEM 12].

Several other vocal features, which are frequent and crucial in debates, are more difficult to capture and their characterization is more subjective such as authority, irony, teasing or disdain. It is also frequent that speakers interrupt each other or speak in parallel to stress their point of view or to show their lack of interest in the other party's perspectives. As a consequence, at the moment, oral transcriptions remain relatively imperfect and partial. Argumentation analysis carried out from these transcriptions should therefore be made with care.

9.2. Argumentation and visual aspects

Non-verbal behaviors, including gazes, facial expressions, gestures and body postures [RIC 08], influence the way a speaker and what is said are perceived. These non-verbal elements of communication, and by extension of argumentation, play a role in dialogues and other types of debates.

Debates frequently take place on TV or on similar media. The contents of the debate and who is talking is clearly central. However, the way the debate is presented to the public and the way speakers and moderators behave may deeply alter several of its features, among which the strength of the arguments, the persuasion effects and elements such as *ad hominem* or expertise considerations. For example, in a TV debate, camera shots and camera angles have an implicit meaning that may alter what the current speaker is saying. Suppose that while speaker A is speaking, the camera is pointing to A's opponent B or at the audience that is laughing or yawning, then what A is saying may be judged to be not as credible as it should have been if the camera had just pointed to him. Speaker A may be supposed to be incompetent or not serious. The same camera can also point to the public, capturing the facial expression of some skeptical listeners. Annotation schemes exist to analyze non-verbal cues, such as the MUMIN coding scheme [ALL 07]. Among other things, the MUMIN framework allows the analysis of who is looking at whom during a conversation, and it could be also used to describe a camera movement.

Besides what the camera shows, the environment of the debate is important: the lighting, the visual perspective, the type of seats, etc. These elements are part of the visual rhetorical dimensions of argumentation. The credibility of the speaker is reinforced by the way he speaks (e.g. clearly, with no hesitation, in a way that is understandable by most listeners), the way he behaves (making gestures or not), the way he is dressed, how and when he looks at the camera or at his opponent, etc. These features are well known to politicians, journalists or businessmen who wish to convince others of their position, perspective, seriousness and commitment.

The background of the room is also important: the type of light, its intensity, the colors of the seats, tables and other furniture, the overall organization of the room, the distance or proximity with the audience, etc. These elements contribute to establishing an atmosphere that may inspire trust in the speaker's ideas or, conversely, suspicion or worry. These elements have been investigated in detail by specialists of communication. They have an intrinsic value, but also depend on the listeners, their level of education, their expectations and their judgment and perception of the speaker.

Besides media, other visual elements are crucial in argumentation. For example, when arguing for a product, its packaging, the colors that are used and even the shape of the package are all important, in particular for food products. These simple visual elements argue much more efficiently and directly than any discourse based on the attractive properties of a product, even if they lead to incorrect evaluations of this product.

Similarly, impressive buildings like justice courts or presidential palaces strongly suggest that the activities realized in these buildings and the competence of its occupants is in harmony with the impressive character of the buildings. A court of justice set in an old, small and ugly building will not have the same effect even if the quality of the judgments which are made are the same as if they were done in a more impressive building.

There are many other visual elements that contribute to an argumentation in our everyday life: company logos, building entrance designs, etc. All these visual elements, either pictures or videos can be annotated, however their interpretation in an argumentation model is complex and contextual.

9.3. Argumentation and sound aspects

Sounds taken in isolation as well as music extracts offer a major contribution to non-verbal argumentation. Sounds are used, for example, to establish a transition between radio programs or to identify them (*jingles*). They can be artificial sounds or concrete sounds such as clocks or whistles. Music is used, for example, in shops, films, sport competitions or in movie trailers. Music used for argumentation purposes is often a short extract of a longer musical work, an extract that includes significant elements such as a melody or a specific rhythm. It can also be a dedicated short piece of music composed for that purpose. This is a frequent case in advertising. Music was also, via non-verbal rhetoric, a powerful means of argumentation, in particular during the Baroque period. Similarly to visual aspects, music has a large diversity of applications in argumentation. Some of the features of music in argumentation and rhetoric are underlined as illustrations to show the wide range of roles music may play.

Music does not convey meaning as language does, it however conveys emotional and symbolic contents that are very important in rhetoric and argumentation. These aspects are often paired with the rational part of arguments in a number of areas and applications. Since music is a more elaborated system than isolated sounds, we focus on music viewed as an organized system of sounds.

9.3.1. *Music and rationality*

Since the Greek period, a number of authors have investigated the structure of music from a rational and scientific point of view. Till the Renaissance, music was part of the *Quadrivium* together with geometry, arithmetics and astronomy. The other three "liberal" arts, the *Trivium*, included grammar, rhetorics and dialectics. Music was the closest discipline to the Trivium. Saint Augustine (354–430, in the *Confessions* and *De Musica*) and Boece (470–525, in the *Consolations*) show that music is a science, via the development of a rational analysis of music based on numbers and proportions, supposed to manage the harmony of movements, including movements of planets. At that period, music was considered not only as a mathematical object describing the structure of melodies and rhythms, with a strong explicative power, but also as a form of abstraction reflecting creativity and perfection. These considerations give an idea of the impact music can have when associated with an argumentative text.

The above elements on music and cognition show that investigating the role of musical activities in rhetoric and argumentation raises several difficulties:

– First, domains in which music operates are not totally clear: psychological, perceptual or emotional. How, then, do these domains interact with textual argumentation?

– A large proportion of musical knowledge that is part of our culture is non-verbal. How is it possible to describe the concrete impact of our musical and sound cultural heritage?

– Next, it is not clear whether musical models can be given a Tarsky-style semantics, independently of any human usage and perception. How is it possible to account for such an abstract and culture-dependent system?

– Finally, music is a multidimensional system that requires several layers of knowledge description and abstraction. Each layer is coherent and reflects a different perspective and system. It is not clear whether these systems elaborate on each other and are consistent or if they are inconsistent or even just unrelated.

9.3.2. *Main features of musical structure: musical knowledge representation*

Music has an organization that is quite different from natural language. The four main levels are, informally:

1) the melody level that accounts for the structure of the "horizontal" dimension of music;

2) the harmony level, which develops the "vertical" level of music in close connection with the melody, by specifying the structure and the sequencing of chords;

3) the polyphony level, which develops the organization of layers of melodies realized by different voices or instruments. Polyphony, which is typical of western music, must observe the rules of harmony and melody construction;

4) the form level, comparable to the discourse or document levels in language, which specifies various musical organizations (e.g. fugue, sonata, scherzo) at a more global level.

Music has many other components that are not discussed here such as timbre and instrumentation, meter and rhythm, dynamics and accentuation, phrasing and articulations, and, in more contemporary music, note clusters, groupings, series, etc. Each of these levels plays an important role in rhetoric and argumentation.

A number of musical elements have been developed through the centuries and have acquired a strong expressive and symbolic power in our western culture. These became major figures of sound that were easily recognized by the audience of the past centuries; they are still used today in various types of music with approximately the same underlying "meaning". These forms are based on principles or expressive constants that borrow from different perceptual considerations and language metaphors.

The main music parameters that must be considered to develop a rhetoric of music and music affect are [SAI 14]:

– modes and tonalities, claimed to have specific colors and to introduce specific moods. For example: the tonality C major is happy, with some idea of fight, pure and innocent, naïve and gentle, in contrast: C minor is sad, grave and serious;

– melodic intervals and profiles of musical motives, in particular in relation with spatial metaphors, also claimed to suggest specific feelings and moods. For example, minor third (1) ascending: sad and painful, (2) descending: calm; major third (1) ascending: happy, joyful, (2) descending: sad;

– melodic development, variations and alternations and musical figures. They are complex systems that must be taken into account. For example, ascending melodic movements (Anabasis, Ascencio) are frequently realized by means of adjacent notes or small intervals, this figure has a positive orientation similarly to orientation metaphors in language where going up is positive;

– rhythm in musical motive, meter, tempo and tempo variations and specific forms of rhythm. These are parameters that can be associated with an immediate perception. Rhythms may be figurative: rhythmic hesitations where a regular rhythm includes gaps with missing notes or a rhythm that progressively disintegrates suggests uncertainty, doubts or anger. Syncopation may also provoke the same kind of feeling because of the instability it suggests with respect to the meter;

– nuances, accentuation and articulation indications, which are as important as in spoken discourse. For example, a loud sound will have a different effect than a very soft one;

– harmony, expressiveness of chords, sequences of chords: these have a role quite similar to tonalities illustrated above;

– timbre, instrumentation and registration for organ: timbre is having a more and more important role in our contemporary civilization. It is formally defined by a weighted combination of harmonics from the fundamental sound. These combinations introduce colors that have an effect on the listener;

– symbolic aspects of forms, proportions in musical motives and numerology. Although these features are more difficult to perceive, they nevertheless have an impact on the listener. For example, a well-balanced melody may entail confidence, whereas a more chaotic structure may entail suspicion or discomfort.

A number of these parameters have received annotation guidelines and norms in music analysis and in information retrieval. It is clear that these parameters largely interact and the moods, affects or feelings produced by a parameter can be further refined, transformed or modified by other parameters. Their association with text is an active research topic. Most of these are still preliminary and under testing. An overview of a number of projects can be found at http://recherche.ircam.fr/equipes/analyse-synthese/peeters/main_techno.php.

9.4. Impact of non-verbal aspects on argument strength and on argument schemes

We have seen in the previous sections, via a number of examples, that non-verbal aspects can have a major influence on argument strength. A sound, music extract or a visual element may reinforce a support or an attack if it has the same tone: positive for supports, negative for attacks. The opposite can also be observed where, for example, a visual aspect contradicts in some way a support or an attack. In that case, these latter are weakened.

It is difficult to precisely evaluate the impact in terms of strength of non-verbal elements since they are objects that are very different from linguistic objects. They have a much more contextual or personal dimension than language whose objects, words and constructions, are more normalized in terms of semantic and pragmatic impact.

Non-verbal elements also have an influence on argument schemes. For example, an argument scheme from expert opinion can be affected if in a video the expert A is arguing with opponents or an audience which is laughing or yawning. In that case, a shift could be observed to an argument scheme based on *ad hominem* considerations, which deeply affects the validity of the argumentation being carried out.

The opposite situation can also be observed for a speaker *a priori* judged to be not very competent. If an audience listens to him with a great attention and approves his arguments, then a shift to an argument scheme based on best explanation can be foreseen.

9.5. Ethical aspects

Ethical aspects related to non-verbal aspects of argumentation are important. While the "textual" part of argumentation essentially relies on language and meaning, which is relatively objective, the non-verbal aspects cannot in general be measured easily and introduce a large part of subjectivity and possible manipulations of an audience.

As illustrated above, a serious argument can be turned into a fallacious argument just by using non-verbal features. Conversely, fallacious arguments may seem, due to a good non-verbal "packaging", to be very well founded and perfectly acceptable. These situations may occur in a large diversity of situations, including those where business, political decisions and advertising are involved. These are in fact part of any human behavior and can seldom be avoided. To circumvent these problems, the rules for a cooperative form of argumentation, as those given in [EEM 01], seem a good approach among a few others. Besides these cooperative rules, research is ongoing in psychological circles on the impact of visual and sound elements on human behavior, which are central to the concerns advocated here.

Bibliography

[ADE 10] ÄDEL A., "Just to give you kind of a map of where we are going: A taxonomy of metadiscourse in spoken and written academic English", *Nordic Journal of English Studies*, vol. 9, no. 2, pp. 69–97, 2010.

[ACH 08] ACHANANUPARP P., HU X., SHEN X., "The evaluation of sentence similarity measures", *International Conference on Data Warehousing and Knowledge Discovery*, Springer, Gothenburg, Sweden, pp. 305–316, 2008.

[AHA 14] AHARONI E., POLNAROV A., LAVEE T. *et al.*, "A benchmark dataset for automatic detection of claims and evidence in the context of controversial topics", *Proceedings of the First Workshop on Argumentation Mining*, Baltimore, MD, Association for Computational Linguistics, pp. 64–68, 2014.

[ALK 16] AL-KHATIB K., WACHSMUTH H., KIESEL J. *et al.*, "A news editorial corpus for mining argumentation strategies", *Proceedings of the 26th International Conference on Computational Linguistics (COLING 16)*, Osaka, Japan, pp. 3433–3443, December 2016.

[ALL 07] ALLWOOD J., CERRATO L., JOKINEN K. *et al.*, "The MUMIN coding scheme for the annotation of feedback, turn management and sequencing phenomena", *Language Resources and Evaluation*, vol. 41, nos 3–4, pp. 273–287, 2007.

[AMO 10] AMOSSY R., *L'argumentation dans le discours*, Armand Colin, Paris, France, 2010.

[AND 10] ANDROUTSOPOULOS I., MALAKASIOTIS P., "A survey of paraphrasing and textual entailment methods", *Journal of Artificial Intelligence Research*, vol. 38, pp. 135–187, 2010.

[ANS 83] ANSCOMBRE J.C., DUCROT O., *L'argumentation dans la langue*, Mardaga, Brussels, Belgium, 1983.

[ART 08] ARTSTEIN R., POESIO M., "Inter-coder agreement for computational linguistics", *Computational Linguistics*, vol. 34, no. 4, 2008.

[AUS 62] AUSTIN J.L., *How to Do Things with Words*, Oxford University Press, Oxford, p. 152, 1962.

[AZA 99] AZAR M., "Argumentative text as rhetorical structure: An application of rhetorical structure theory", *Argumentation*, vol. 13, no. 1, pp. 97–114, 1999.

[BAR 16] BARKER E., GAIZAUSKAS R., "Summarizing multi-party argumentative conversations in reader comment on news", *Proceedings of the 3rd Workshop on Argument Mining*, Association for Computational Linguistics, Berlin, Germany, pp. 12–20, 2016.

[BEX 12] BEX F., GORDON T., LAWRENCE J. *et al.*, "Interchanging arguments between Carneades and AIF", *Computational Models of Argument (COMMA)*, vol. 245, pp. 390–397, 2012.

[BIR 11] BIRAN O., RAMBOW O., "Identifying justifications in written dialogs by classifying text as argumentative", *International Journal of Semantic Computing*, vol. 5, no. 4, pp. 363–381, 2011.

[BLA 07] BLAIR-GOLDENSOHN S., MCKEOWN K., RAMBOW O., "Building and refining rhetorical-semantic relation models", *Human Language Technologies 2007: The Conference of the North American Chapter of the Association for Computational Linguistics; Proceedings of the Main Conference*, Rochester, NY, pp. 428–435, April 2007.

[BOJ 01] BOJARCZUKA C.C., LOPESB H.S., FREITASC A.A., "Data mining with constrained-syntax genetic programming: Applications in medical data set", *Algorithms*, vol. 6, p. 7, 2001.

[BOL 14] BOLTUI F., NAJDER J., "Back up your stance: recognizing arguments in online discussions", *Proceedings of the First Workshop on Argumentation Mining*, Association for Computational Linguistics, Baltimore, MD, pp. 49–58, 2014.

[BUD 11] BUDZYNSKA K., REED C., Whence Inference, Report, University of Dundee, Scotland, 2011.

[BUD 14a] BUDZYNSKA K., JANIER M., KANG J. *et al.*, "Towards argument mining from dialogue", *Computational Models of Argument, Proceedings of COMMA 2014, in Frontiers in Artificial Intelligence and Applications*, vol. 266, IOS Press, Amsterdam, pp. 185–196, 2014.

[BUD 14b] BUDZYNSKA K., JANIER M., REED C. *et al.*, "A model for processing illocutionary structures and argumentation in debates", *Proceedings of LREC14*, Reykjavik, Iceland, 2014.

[BUD 14c] BUDZYNSKA K., ROCCI A., YASKORSKA O., "Financial dialogue games: A protocol for earnings conference calls", *Computational Models of Argument, Proceedings of COMMA 2014, Frontiers in Artificial Intelligence and Applications*, vol. 266, IOS Press, Amsterdam, pp. 19–30, 2014.

[BUD 16] BUDZYNSKA K., JANIER M., REED C. *et al.*, "Theoretical foundations for illocutionary structure parsing", *Argument & Computation*, vol. 7, no. 1, pp. 91–108, 2016.

[BUD 18] BUDZYNSKA K., PEREIRA-FARINA M., DE FRANCO D. *et al.*, "Time-constrained multi-layer corpus creation", *16th ArgDiap Conference Book of Abstracts*, Warsaw, Poland, pp. 31–36, 2018.

[CAB 12] CABRIO E., VILLATA S., "Combining textual entailment and argumentation theory for supporting online debates interactions", *Proceedings of the 50th Annual Meeting of the Association for Computational Linguistics: Short Papers - Volume 2*, ACL '12, Association for Computational Linguistics, Stroudsburg, PA, pp. 208–212, 2012.

[CAB 13] CABRIO E., VILLATA S., "A natural language bipolar argumentation approach to support users in online debate interactions", *Argument and Computation*, vol. 4, no. 3, pp. 209–230, 2013.

[CAR 03] CARLSON L., MARCU D., OKUROWSKI M.E., "Building a discourse-tagged corpus in the framework of rhetorical structure theory", *Current and New Directions in Discourse and Dialogue*, Springer, Dordrecht, Netherlands, pp. 85–112, 2003.

[CHA 06] CHANG D.-S., CHOI K.-S., "Incremental cue phrase learning and bootstrapping method for causality extraction using cue phrase and word pair probabilities", *Information Processing & Management*, vol. 42, no. 3, pp. 662–678, 2006.

[CHE 06] CHESVEÑAR C., MCGINNIS J., MODGIL S. *et al.*, "Towards an argument interchange format", *The Knowledge Engineering Review*, vol. 21, no. 4, pp. 293–316, 2006.

[CHO 00] CHOI F.Y.Y., "Advances in domain independent linear text segmentation", *Proceedings of the 1st North American chapter of the Association for Computational Linguistics Conference*, Seattle, WA, pp. 26–33, 2000.

[COR 04] CORELLA J., SPENCER S., ZANNAB M., "An affirmed self and an open mind: Self-affirmation and sensitivity to argument strength", *Journal of Experimental Social Psychology*, vol. 40, no. 3, pp. 350–356, 2004.

[CRU 86] CRUSE A., *Lexical Semantics*, Cambridge University Press, Cambridge, 1986.

[DUS 17] DUSMANU M., CABRIO E., VILLATA S., "Argument mining on Twitter: Arguments, facts and sources", *The 2017 Conference on Empirical Methods in Natural Language Processing, EMNLP 2017*, Copenhagen, Denmark, September 2017.

[EEM 82] VAN EEMEREN F.H., GROOTENDORST R., "The speech acts of arguing and convincing in externalized discussions", *Journal of Pragmatics*, vol. 6, no. 1, pp. 1–24, 1982.

[EEM 92] VAN EEMEREN F., GROTENDORST R., *Argumentation, Communication and Fallacies*, Lawrence Erlbaum, Mahwah, NJ, 1992.

[EEM 01] VAN EEMEREN F., GROTENDORST R., SNOECK HENKEMANS F., *Argumentation, Analysis, Evaluation, Presentation*, Routledge, Abingdon-on-Thames, 2001.

[EEM 03] VAN EEMEREN F.H., HOUTLOSSER P., "The development of the pragma-dialectical approach to argumentation", *Argumentation*, vol. 17, pp. 387–403, 2003.

[EGE 17] EGER S., DAXENBERGER J., GUREVYCH I., "Neural end-to-end learning for computational argumentation mining", *CoRR*, abs/1704.06104, 2017.

[FAU 14] FAULKNER A., "Automated classification of stance in student essays: an approach using stance target information and the Wikipedia link-based measure", *The Twenty-Seventh International Florida Artificial Intelligence Research Society (FLAIRS) Conference*, Pensacola Beach, FL, 2014.

[FEN 11] FENG V., HIRST G., "Classifying arguments by scheme", *Proceedings of 49th ACL: Human Language Technologies*, Portland, OR, 2011.

[FIE 07] FIEDLER A., HORACEK H., "Argumentation within deductive reasoning", *Journal of Intelligent Systems*, vol. 22, no. 1, pp. 49–70, 2007.

[FLE 71] FLEISS J.L., "Measuring nominal scale agreement among many raters", *Psychological Bulletin*, vol. 76, no. 5, p. 378, 1971.

[FRE 11] FREEMAN J.B., *Argument Structure: Representation and Theory*, Springer Science & Business Media, Berlin, Germany, vol. 18, p. 154, 2011.

[GET 05] GETOOR L., DIEHL C.P., "Link mining: A survey", *Acm Sigkdd Explorations Newsletter*, vol. 7, no. 2, pp. 3–12, 2005.

[GHO 13] GHOSH D., MURESAN S., WACHOLDER N. *et al.*, "Analyzing argumentative discourse units in online interactions", *ACL 2013, Proceedings of the First Workshop on Argumentation Mining*, ACL, Baltimore, ML, pp. 39–48, 2013.

[GOT 14] GOTTIPATI S., QIU M., YANG L. *et al.*, "An integrated model for user attribute discovery: A case study on political affiliation identification", *Pacific-Asia Conference on Knowledge Discovery and Data Mining*, Springer, Hyderabad, India, pp. 434–446, 2014.

[GOU 14] GOUDAS T., LOUIZOS C., PETASIS G. *et al.*, "Argument extraction from news, blogs, and social media", *Hellenic Conference on Artificial Intelligence*, Springer, Ioannina, Greece, pp. 41–58, 2014.

[GRA 11] GRASSO F., HAM J., MASTHOFF J., "User models for motivational systems – the affective and the rational routes to persuasion", *Advances in User Modeling – UMAP 2011 Workshops*, 2011.

[GRE 17] GREEN N., "Manual identification of arguments with implicit conclusions using semantic rules for argument mining", *EMNLP17, Workshop on Argument Mining*, 2017.

[GRI 75] GRICE H.P., "Logic and conversation", in COLE P., MORGAN J. (eds), *Syntax and Semantics*, vol. 3, Academic Press, Cambridge, MA, pp. 41–58, 1975.

[GRI 90] GRIZE J.B., *Logique et Langage*, Ophryx, Paris, France, 1990.

[HAB 87] HABERMAS J., *Theory of Communicative Action, Volume Two: Lifeworld and System: A Critique of Functionalist Reason*, Translated by Thomas A. McCarthy, Beacon Press, Boston, MA, 1987.

[HAB 14] HABERNAL I., Argumentation in user-generated content: annotation guidelines, Ubiquitous Knowledge Processing Lab (UKP Lab) Computer Science Department, Technische Universität Darmstadt, 2014.

[HAB 17] HABERNAL I., GUREVYCH I., "Argumentation mining in user-generated web discourse", *Computational Linguistics*, vol. 43, no. 1, pp. 125–179, 2017.

[HER 10] HERNAULT H., BOLLEGALA D., ISHIZUKA M., "Towards semi-supervised classification of discourse relations using feature correlations", *Proceedings of the 11th Annual Meeting of the Special Interest Group on Discourse and Dialogue*, Association for Computational Linguistics, Tokyo, Japan, pp. 55–58, 2010.

[HIT 06] HITCHCOCK D., VERHEIJ B., *Arguing on the Toulmin Model*, Springer, New York, 2006.

[HOF 14] HOFFMANN M., BORENSTEIN J., "Understanding ill-structured engineering ethics problems through a collaborative learning and argument visualization approach", *Science and Engineering Ethics*, vol. 20, no. 1, pp. 261–276, 2014.

[HOF 15] HOFFMANN M.H., LINGLE J.A., "Facilitating problem-based learning by means of collaborative argument visualization software in advance", *Teaching Philosophy*, vol. 38, no. 4, pp. 371–398, 2015.

[HOU 13] HOUY C., NIESEN T., FETTKE P. *et al.*, "Towards automated identification and analysis of argumentation structures in the decision corpus of the German Federal Constitutional Court", *2013 7th IEEE International Conference on Digital Ecosystems and Technologies (DEST)*, IEEE, Menlo Park, CA, pp. 72–77, 2013.

[JAN 14] JANIER M., LAWRENCE J., REED C., "OVA+: An argument analysis interface", *Computational Models of Argument: Proceedings of COMMA*, vol. 266, pp. 463–464, Pitlochry, Scotland, 2014.

[JAN 16] JANIER M., REED C., "Corpus resources for dispute mediation discourse", *Proceedings of the Tenth International Conference on Language Resources and Evaluation (LREC 2016)*, pp. 1014–1021, 2016.

[KAN 14] KANG J., SAINT-DIZIER P., "A discourse grammar for processing arguments in context", *Computational Models of Argument, Proceedings of COMMA 2014, Frontiers in Artificial Intelligence and Applications*, vol. 266, IOS Press, Amsterdam, pp. 43–50, 2014.

[KIM 14] KIM Y., "Convolutional neural networks for sentence classification", *Proceedings of the 2014 Conference on Empirical Methods in Natural Language Processing (EMNLP)*, pp. 1746–1751, 2014.

[KON 16] KONAT B., BUDZYNSKA K., SAINT-DIZIER P., "Rephrase in argument structure", *Proceedings of the Foundations of the Language of Argumentation (FLA) Workshop*, pp. 32–39, 2016.

[KRI 04] KRIPPENDORFF K., "Reliability in content analysis", *Human Communication Research*, vol. 30, no. 3, pp. 411–433, 2004.

[LAN 77] LANDIS J.R., KOCH G.G., "The measurement of observer agreement for categorical data", *Biometrics*, vol. 33, no. 1, pp. 159–174, 1977.

[LAW 12] LAWRENCE J., BEX F., REED C. *et al.*, "AIFdb: Infrastructure for the argument web", in VERHEIJ B., SZEIDER S., WOLTRAN S. (eds), *Computational Models of Argument, Proceedings of COMMA 2012, Frontiers in Artificial Intelligence and Applications*, vol. 245, IOS Press, Amsterdam, pp. 515–516, 2012.

[LAW 15] LAWRENCE J., JANIER M., REED C., "Working with open argument corpora", *European Conference on Argumentation (ECA)*, 2015.

[LAW 16] LAWRENCE J., REED C., "Argument mining using argumentation scheme structures", *Computational Models of Argument, Proceedings from COMMA 2016, Frontiers in Artificial Intelligence and Applications*, vol. 287, IOS Press, Amsterdam, pp. 379–390, 2016.

[LEM 12] LEMKE J.L., "Analyzing verbal data: Principles, methods, and problems", *Second International Handbook of Science Education*, pp. 1471–1484, Springer, New York, 2012.

[LIE 16] LIEBECK M., ESAU K., CONRAD S., "What to do with an airport? Mining arguments in the German Online Participation Project Tempelhofer Feld", *Proceedings of the Third Workshop on Argument Mining (ArgMining2016)*, pp. 144–153, 2016.

[LIN 09] LIN Z., KAN M.-Y., NG H.T., "Recognizing implicit discourse relations in the Penn Discourse Treebank", *Proceedings of the 2009 Conference on Empirical Methods in Natural Language Processing*, pp. 343–351, 2009.

[LIP 15] LIPPI M., TORRONI P., "Context-independent claim detection for argument mining", *Twenty-Fourth International Joint Conference on Artificial Intelligence*, Buenos Aires, Argentina, 2015.

[LIP 16] LIPPI M., TORRONI P., "Argumentation mining: State of the art and emerging trends", *ACM Transactions on Internet Technology*, vol. 16, no. 2, pp. 10:1–10:25, March 2016.

[LLE 14] LLEWELLYN C., GROVER C., OBERLANDER J. *et al.*, "Re-using an argument corpus to aid in the curation of social media collections", CHAIR N. C.C., CHOUKRI K., DECLERCK T. *et al.* (eds), *Proceedings of the Ninth International Conference on Language Resources and Evaluation (LREC'14)*, European Language Resources Association (ELRA), Reykjavik, Iceland, 2014.

[MAN 88] MANN W.C., THOMSON S.A., "Rhetorical Structure Theory: Toward a functional theory of text organization", *Text*, vol. 8, no. 3, pp. 243–281, 1988.

[MAN 01] MANI I., *The Generative Lexicon*, John Benjamins Publishing, Amsterdam, Netherlands, 2001.

[MAN 03] MANI I., SCHIFFMAN B., ZHANG J., "Inferring temporal ordering of events in news", *Companion Volume of the Proceedings of HLT-NAACL 2003-Short Papers*, Edmonton, Canada, 2003.

[MAR 99] MARCU D., "A decision-based approach to rhetorical parsing", *Proceedings of the 37th Annual Meeting of the Association for Computational Linguistics*, College Park, Maryland, 1999.

[MAR 02] MARCU D., ECHIHABI A., "An unsupervised approach to recognizing discourse relations", *Proceedings of the 40th Annual Meeting of the Association for Computational Linguistics*, Philadelphia, Pennsylvania, 2002.

[MOC 09] MOCHALES PALAU R., MOENS M.-F., "Argumentation mining: The detection, classification and structure of arguments in text", *Proceedings of the 12th ICAIL*, Barcelona, Spain, 2009.

[MOC 11] MOCHALES R., MOENS M.-F., "Argumentation mining", *Artificial Intelligence and Law*, vol. 19, no. 1, pp. 1–22, 2011.

[MOE 85] MOESCHLER J., *Argumentation et conversation*, Hatier, Paris, France, 1985.

[MOE 07] MOENS M.-F., BOIY E., MOCHALES PALAU R. *et al.*, "Automatic detection of arguments in legal texts", *ICAIL '07*, pp. 225–230, 2007.

[MUN 88] MUNCH J., SWASY J., "Rhetorical question, summarization frequency, and argument strength effects on recall", *Journal of Consumer Research*, vol. 15, no. 1, pp. 69–76, 1988.

[MUS 16] MUSI E., GHOSH D., MURESAN S., "Towards feasible guidelines for the annotation of argument schemes", *Proceedings of the Third Workshop on Argument Mining, hosted by the 54th Annual Meeting of the Association for Computational Linguistics, ArgMining@ACL 2016, August 12,* The Association for Computer Linguistics, Berlin, Germany, 2016.

[NAD 07] NADEAU D., SEKINE S., "A survey of named entity recognition and classification", *Lingvisticae Investigationes*, vol. 30, no. 1, pp. 3–26, 2007.

[NEW 91] NEWMAN S., MARSHALL C., Pushing Toulmin too far: Learning from an argument representation scheme, Technical Report SSL-92, Xerox PARC, Palo Alto, CA, 1991.

[NGU 07] NGUYEN N., GUO Y., "Comparisons of sequence labeling algorithms and extensions", *Proceedings of the 24th International Conference on Machine Learning*, ACM, Corvallis, OR, pp. 681–688, 2007.

[NGU 15] NGUYEN H., LITMAN D., "Extracting argument and domain words for identifying argument components in texts", *Proceedings of 2nd Workshop on Argumentation Mining*, Denver, CO, 2015.

[NGU 17] NGUYEN Q.V.H., DUONG C.T., NGUYEN T.T. *et al.*, "Argument discovery via crowdsourcing", *The VLDB Journal*, vol. 26, no. 4, pp. 511–535, 2017.

[ODO 00] O'DONNELL M., "RSTTool 2.4–a markup tool for rhetorical structure theory", *INLG'2000 Proceedings of the First International Conference on Natural Language Generation*, Mitzpe Ramon, Israel, 2000.

[OKE 77] O'KEEFE D.J., "Two concepts of arguments", *The Journal of the American Forensic Association*, vol. XIII, no. 3, pp. 121–128, 1977.

[OKA 08] OKADA A., BUCKINGHAM SHUM S., SHERBONE T. (eds), *Knowledge Cartography: Software Tools and Mapping Techniques*, Springer, New York, 2008.

[PAR 08] PARSONS S., ATKINSON S., HAIGH K., LEVITT K. *et al.*, "Argument schemes for reasoning about trust", *Computational Models of Argument, Proceedings of COMMA 2008, Frontiers in Artificial Intelligence and Applications*, vol. 172, IOS Press, Amsterdam, pp. 285–296, 2008.

[PAR 14] PARK J., CARDIE C., "Identifying appropriate support for propositions in online user comments", *Proceedings of the First Workshop on Argument Mining, hosted by the 52nd Annual Meeting of the Association for Computational Linguistics, ArgMining@ACL 2014, June 26, 2014,* The Association for Computer Linguistics, Baltimore, MD, pp. 29–38, 2014.

[PEL 13] PELDSZUS A., STEDE M., "From argument diagrams to argumentation mining in texts: A survey", *International Journal of Cognitive Informatics and Natural Intelligence (IJCINI)*, vol. 7, no. 1, pp. 1–31, 2013.

[PEL 14] PELDSZUS A., "Towards segment-based recognition of argumentation structure in short texts", *Proceedings of the First Workshop on Argumentation Mining*, Association for Computational Linguistics, Baltimore, MD, pp. 88–97, 2014.

[PER 58] PERELMAN C., OLBRECHTS TYTECA L., *The New Rhetoric: A Treatise on Argumentation*, University of Notre Dame Press, Notre Dame, IN, 1958.

[PER 77] PERELMAN C., *L'empire Rhétorique*, Vrin, Paris, France, 1977.

[PER 80] PEREIRA F., WARREN D., "Definite clause grammars for language analysis–a survey of the formalism and a comparison with augmented transition networks", *Artificial Intelligence*, vol. 13, pp. 231–278, 1980.

[PLA 96] PLANTIN C., *L'argumentation*, Le Seuil, Paris, France, 1996.

[POL 95] POLLOCK J.L., *Cognitive Carpentry: A Blueprint for How to Build a Person*, MIT Press, Cambridge, MA, 1995.

[POT 17] POTASH P., ROMANOV A., RUMSHISKY A., "Here's my point: Joint pointer architecture for argument mining", *Proceedings of the 2017 Conference on Empirical Methods in Natural Language Processing, EMNLP 2017*, September 9–11, 2017, Copenhagen, Denmark, pp. 1364–1373, 2017.

[PUS 86] PUSTEJOVSKY J., *The Generative Lexicon*, MIT Press, Cambridge, MA, 1986.

[RAH 09] RAHWAN I., REED C., "The argument interchange format", SIMARI G.R., RAHWAN I. (eds), *Argumentation in Artificial Intelligence*, pp. 383–402, Springer, New York, 2009.

[RAJ 16] RAJENDRAN P., BOLLEGALA D., PARSONS S., "Contextual stance classification of opinions: A step towards enthymeme reconstruction in online reviews", *Proceedings of the Third Workshop on Argument Mining (ArgMining2016)*, pp. 31–39, 2016.

[REE 04] REED C., ROWE G., "Araucaria: Software for argument analysis, diagramming and representation", *International Journal of AI Tools*, vol. 14, pp. 961–980, 2004.

[REE 06] REED C., "Preliminary results from an argument corpus", Bermúdez E.M., Miyares L.R. (eds), *Linguistics in the Twenty-first Century*, Scholars Press, Riga, Latvia, pp. 185–196, 2006.

[REE 08a] REED C., MOCHALES PALAU R., ROWE G. *et al.*, "Language Resources for Studying Argument", *Proceedings of the 6th conference on Language Resources and Evaluation-LREC 2008*, pp. 91–100, 2008.

[REE 08b] REED C., WELLS S., DEVEREUX J. *et al.*, "AIF+: Dialogue in the Argument Interchange Format", *Frontiers in Artificial Intelligence and Applications*, vol. 172, p. 311, 2008.

[REE 17] REED C., BUDZYNSKA K., DUTHIE R. *et al.*, "The Argument Web: An online ecosystem of tools, systems and services for argumentation", *Philosophy & Technology*, vol. 30, no. 2, pp. 137–160, 2017.

[REI 14] REISERT P., MIZUNO J., KANNO M. *et al.*, "A corpus study for identifying evidence on microblogs", *Proceedings of LAW VIII-The 8th Linguistic Annotation Workshop*, pp. 70–74, 2014.

[RIC 08] RICHMOND V.P., MCCROSKEY J.C., HICKSON M., *Nonverbal Behavior in Interpersonal Relations*, Allyn & Bacon, Boston, MA, USA, 2008.

[RIN 15] RINOTT R., DANKIN L., PEREZ C.A. *et al.*, "Show me your evidence - an automatic method for context dependent evidence detection", in *Proceedings of the 2015 Conference on Empirical Methods in Natural Language Processing*, Lisbon, Portugal, pp. 440–450, 2015.

[ROS 12] ROSENTHAL S., MCKEOWN K., "Detecting opinionated claims in online discussions", *Sixth IEEE International Conference on Semantic Computing, ICSC 2012*, September 19–21, 2012, Palermo, Italy, pp. 30–37, 2012.

[ROU 84] ROULET E., "Speech acts, discourse structure and pragmatic connectives", *Journal of Pragmatics*, vol. 8, pp. 31–47, 1984.

[SAI 12] SAINT-DIZIER P., "Processing natural language arguments with the TextCoop platform", *Journal of Argumentation and Computation*, vol. 3, no. 1, pp. 49–82, 2012.

[SAI 14] SAINT-DIZIER P., *Musical Rhetoric: Foundations and Annotation Schemes*, ISTE Ltd, London and John Wiley & Sons, New York, 2014.

[SAI 16a] SAINT-DIZIER P., "The bottleneck of knowledge and language resources", *Proceedings of LREC16*, Portorož, Slovenia, 2016.

[SAI 16b] SAINT-DIZIER P., "Challenges of argument mining: Generating an argument synthesis based on the qualia structure", *Proceedings of INLG16*, Edinburgh, Scotland, 2016.

[SAI 17] SAINT-DIZIER P., "Knowledge-driven argument mining based on the qualia structure", *Journal of Argumentation and Computation*, vol. 8, no. 2, pp. 193–210, 2017.

[SAI 18] SAINT-DIZIER P., "A knowledge-based approach to warrant induction", *Computational Models of Argument, Proceedings of COMMA 2018, Frontiers in Artificial Intelligence*, vol. 305, IOS Press, Amsterdam, p. 289, 2018.

[SAR 15] SARDIANOS C., KATAKIS I.M., PETASIS G. *et al.*, "Argument extraction from news", *Proceedings of the 2nd Workshop on Argumentation Mining*, pp. 56–66, 2015.

[SAU 06] SAURÍ R., LITTMAN J., KNIPPEN B. *et al.*, "TimeML annotation guidelines", *Version*, vol. 1, no. 1, p. 31, 2006.

[SCH 80] SCHIFFRIN D., "Meta-talk: Organizational and evaluative brackets in discourse", *Sociological Inquiry*, vol. 50, pp. 199–236, 1980.

[SCH 12] SCHNEIDER J., WYNER A.Z., "Identifying consumers' arguments in text", *SWAIE*, pp. 31–42, 2012.

[SCH 13] SCHNEIDER J., SAMP K., PASSANT A. *et al.*, "Arguments about deletion: How experience improves the acceptability of arguments in ad-hoc online task groups", *Proceedings of the 2013 Conference on Computer Supported Cooperative Work*, CSCW'13, ACM, New York, NY, pp. 1069–1080, 2013.

[SEA 69] SEARLE J.R., *Speech Acts, An Essay in the Philosophy of Language*, Cambridge University Press, Cambridge, 1969.

[SEA 85] SEARLE J.R., VANDERVEKEN D., *Foundations of Illocutionary Logic*, Cambridge University Press, Cambridge, 1985.

[SEL 85] SELLS P., *Lectures on Contemporary Syntactic Theories*, CSLI Series, vol. 3, Stanford University, Stanford, CA, 1985.

[SHI 86] SHIEBER S., *An Introduction to Unification-Based Approaches to Grammar*, CSLI Series vol. 4, Stanford University, Stanford, CA, 1986.

[STA 14] STAB C., GUREVYCH I., "Annotating argument components and relations in persuasive essays", *Proceedings of COLING 2014, the 25th International Conference on Computational Linguistics: Technical Papers*, Dublin, Ireland, pp. 1501–1510, 2014.

[STA 15] STAB C., GUREVYCH I., Guidelines for annotating argumentation structures in persuasive essays, Ubiquitous Knowledge Processing Lab (UKP Lab) Computer Science Department, Technische Universität Darmstadt, May 2015.

[STA 17] STAB C., GUREVYCH I., "Parsing argumentation structures in persuasive essays", *Computational Linguistics*, vol. 43, no. 3, pp. 619–659, 2017.

[STE 00] STENT A., "Rhetorical structure in dialog", *Proceedings of the First International Conference on Narural Language Generation*, Association for Computational Linguistics, Mitzpe Ramon, Israel, vol. 14, pp. 247–252, 2000.

[STE 12] STENETORP P., PYYSALO S., TOPI G. *et al.*, "BRAT: A web-based tool for NLP-assisted text annotation", *Proceedings of the Demonstrations at the 13th Conference of the European Chapter of the Association for Computational Linguistics*, Association for Computational Linguistics, Stroudsburg, PA, pp. 102–107, 2012.

[SWA 15] SWANSON R., ECKER B., WALKER M., "Argument mining: Extracting arguments from online dialogue", *Proceedings of SIGDIAL15*, Prague, Czech Republic, 2015.

[TER 18] TERUEL M., CARDELLINO C., CARDELLINO F. *et al.*, "Increasing argument annotation reproducibility by using inter-annotator agreement to improve guidelines", *Proceedings of the Eleventh International Conference on Language Resources and Evaluation (LREC-2018)*, Miyazaki, Japan, 2018.

[TEU 99a] TEUFEL S. *et al.*, Argumentative zoning: Information extraction from scientific text, PhD Thesis, Citeseer, 1999.

[TEU 99b] TEUFEL S., CARLETTA J., MOENS M., "An annotation scheme for discourse-level argumentation in research articles", *Proceedings of the Ninth Conference on European Chapter of the Association for Computational Linguistics*, EACL '99, Association for Computational Linguistics, Stroudsburg, PA, pp. 110–117, 1999.

[TEU 02] TEUFEL S., MOENS M., "Summarizing scientific articles: Experiments with relevance and rhetorical status", *Computational linguistics*, vol. 28, no. 4, pp. 409–445, 2002.

[TOU 03] TOULMIN S., *The Uses of Argument*, Cambridge University Press, Cambridge, 2003.

[VAN 07] VAN GELDER T., "The rationale for Rationale", *Law, Probability and Risk*, vol. 6, nos 1–4, pp. 23–42, 2007.

[VIL 12] VILLALBA M.G., SAINT-DIZIER P., "Some facets of argument mining for opinion analysis", *Computational Models of Argument, Proceedings of COMMA 2012, Frontiers in Artificial Intelligence and Applicaitons*, vol. 245, IOS Publishing, Amsterdam, pp. 23–34, 2012.

[VIS 18] Visser J., Duthie R., Lawrence J. *et al.*, "Intertextual correspondence for integrating corpora", *Proceedings of the Eleventh International Conference on Language Resources and Evaluation (LREC-2018)*, Miyazaki, Japan, 2018.

[WAC 14] Wacholder N., Muresan S., Ghosh D. *et al.*, "Annotating multiparty discourse: Challenges for agreement metrics", *Proceedings of the 8th Linguistic Annotation Workshop, 2014, August 23–24*, Dublin, Ireland, 2014.

[WAC 17] Wachsmuth H., Naderi N., Hou Y. *et al.*, "Computational argumentation quality assessment in natural language", *Proceedings of the 15th Conference of the European Chapter of the Association for Computational Linguistics*, Valencia, Spain, pp. 176–187, April 2017.

[WAL 96] Walton D., *Argumentation Schemes for Presumptive Reasoning*, L. Erlbaum Associates, New York, NY, 1996.

[WAL 08] Walton D., Reed C., Macagno F., *Argumentation Schemes*, Cambridge University Press, Cambridge, 2008.

[WAL 12] Walker M., Anand P., Abbot R., "A corpus for research on deliberation and debate", *Proceedings of LREC 2012*, Istanbul, Turkey, 2012.

[WAL 15a] Walton D., *Goal-Based Reasoning for Argumentation*, Cambridge University Press, Cambridge, 2015.

[WAL 15b] Walton D., Macagno F., "A classification system for argumentation schemes", *Argument & Computation*, vol. 6, no. 3, pp. 219–245, 2015.

[WIE 87] Wierzbicka A., *English Speech Act Verbs: A Semantic Dictionary*, Academic Press, Cambridge, MA, 1987.

[ZHA 03] Zhang D., Lee W.S., "Question classification using support vector machines", *SIGIR 03 Proceedings of the 26th annual international ACM SIGIR conference on Research and development in information retrieval*, ACM, Toronto, Canada, pp. 26–32, 2003.

[ZHA 11] Zhao X., Strasser A., Cappella J.N. *et al.*, "A measure of perceived argument strength: reliability and validity", *Communication Methods and Measures*, vol. 5, no. 1, pp. 48–75, 2011.

[ZUK 00] Zukerman I., Roger M., Korb K., "Using argumentation strategies in automatic argument generation", *Proceedings of INLG 2000*, Mitzpe Ramon, Israel, 2000.

Index

Other titles from

in

Information Systems, Web and Pervasive Computing

2019

ALBAN Daniel, EYNAUD Philippe, MALAURENT Julien, RICHET Jean-Loup, VITARI Claudio
Information Systems Management: Governance, Urbanization and Alignment

AUGEY Dominique, with the collaboration of ALCARAZ Marina
Digital Information Ecosystems: Smart Press

BATTON-HUBERT Mireille, DESJARDIN Eric, PINET François
Geographic Data Imperfection 1: From Theory to Applications

BRIQUET-DUHAZÉ Sophie, TURCOTTE Catherine
From Reading-Writing Research to Practice

BROCHARD Luigi, KAMATH Vinod, CORBALAN Julita, HOLLAND Scott, MITTELBACH Walter, OTT Michael
Energy-Efficient Computing and Data Centers

CHAMOUX Jean-Pierre
The Digital Era 2: Political Economy Revisited

GAUCHEREL Cédric, GOUYON Pierre-Henri, DESSALLES Jean-Louis
Information, The Hidden Side of Life

GHLALA Riadh
Analytic SQL in SQL Server 2014/2016

SOURIS Marc
Epidemiology and Geography: Principles, Methods and Tools of Spatial Analysis

TOUNSI Wiem
Cyber-Vigilance and Digital Trust: Cyber Security in the Era of Cloud Computing and IoT

2018

ARDUIN Pierre-Emmanuel
Insider Threats
(Advances in Information Systems Set – Volume 10)

CARMÈS Maryse
Digital Organizations Manufacturing: Scripts, Performativity and Semiopolitics
(Intellectual Technologies Set – Volume 5)

CARRÉ Dominique, VIDAL Geneviève
Hyperconnectivity: Economical, Social and Environmental Challenges
(Computing and Connected Society Set – Volume 3)

CHAMOUX Jean-Pierre
The Digital Era 1: Big Data Stakes

DOUAY Nicolas
Urban Planning in the Digital Age
(Intellectual Technologies Set – Volume 6)

FABRE Renaud, BENSOUSSAN Alain
The Digital Factory for Knowledge: Production and Validation of Scientific Results

GAUDIN Thierry, LACROIX Dominique, MAUREL Marie-Christine, POMEROL Jean-Charles
Life Sciences, Information Sciences

GAYARD Laurent
Darknet: Geopolitics and Uses
(Computing and Connected Society Set – Volume 2)

IAFRATE Fernando
Artificial Intelligence and Big Data: The Birth of a New Intelligence
(Advances in Information Systems Set – Volume 8)

LE DEUFF Olivier
Digital Humanities: History and Development
(Intellectual Technologies Set – Volume 4)

MANDRAN Nadine
Traceable Human Experiment Design Research: Theoretical Model and Practical Guide
(Advances in Information Systems Set – Volume 9)

PIVERT Olivier
NoSQL Data Models: Trends and Challenges

ROCHET Claude
Smart Cities: Reality or Fiction

SAUVAGNARGUES Sophie
Decision-making in Crisis Situations: Research and Innovation for Optimal Training

SEDKAOUI Soraya
Data Analytics and Big Data

SZONIECKY Samuel
Ecosystems Knowledge: Modeling and Analysis Method for Information and Communication
(Digital Tools and Uses Set – Volume 6)

2017

BOUHAÏ Nasreddine, SALEH Imad
Internet of Things: Evolutions and Innovations
(Digital Tools and Uses Set – Volume 4)

BOUVARD Patricia, SUZANNE Hervé
Collective Intelligence Development in Business

EL FALLAH SEGHROUCHNI Amal, ISHIKAWA Fuyuki, HÉRAULT Laurent,
TOKUDA Hideyuki
Enablers for Smart Cities

FABRE Renaud, in collaboration with MESSERSCHMIDT-MARIET Quentin,
HOLVOET Margot
New Challenges for Knowledge

GAUDIELLO Ilaria, ZIBETTI Elisabetta
Learning Robotics, with Robotics, by Robotics
(Human-Machine Interaction Set – Volume 3)

HENROTIN Joseph
The Art of War in the Network Age
(Intellectual Technologies Set – Volume 1)

KITAJIMA Munéo
Memory and Action Selection in Human–Machine Interaction
(Human–Machine Interaction Set – Volume 1)

LAGRAÑA Fernando
E-mail and Behavioral Changes: Uses and Misuses of Electronic
Communications

LEIGNEL Jean-Louis, UNGARO Thierry, STAAR Adrien
Digital Transformation
(Advances in Information Systems Set – Volume 6)

NOYER Jean-Max
Transformation of Collective Intelligences
(Intellectual Technologies Set – Volume 2)

VENTRE Daniel
Information Warfare – 2nd edition

VITALIS André
The Uncertain Digital Revolution
(Computing and Connected Society Set – Volume 1)

2015

ARDUIN Pierre-Emmanuel, GRUNDSTEIN Michel, ROSENTHAL-SABROUX Camille
Information and Knowledge System
(Advances in Information Systems Set – Volume 2)

BÉRANGER Jérôme
Medical Information Systems Ethics

BRONNER Gérald
Belief and Misbelief Asymmetry on the Internet

IAFRATE Fernando
From Big Data to Smart Data
(Advances in Information Systems Set – Volume 1)

KRICHEN Saoussen, BEN JOUIDA Sihem
Supply Chain Management and its Applications in Computer Science

NEGRE Elsa
Information and Recommender Systems
(Advances in Information Systems Set – Volume 4)

POMEROL Jean-Charles, EPELBOIN Yves, THOURY Claire
MOOCs

SALLES Maryse
Decision-Making and the Information System
(Advances in Information Systems Set – Volume 3)

SAMARA Tarek
ERP and Information Systems: Integration or Disintegration
(Advances in Information Systems Set – Volume 5)

2014

DINET Jérôme
Information Retrieval in Digital Environments

HÉNO Raphaële, CHANDELIER Laure
3D Modeling of Buildings: Outstanding Sites

KEMBELLEC Gérald, CHARTRON Ghislaine, SALEH Imad
Recommender Systems

MATHIAN Hélène, SANDERS Lena
Spatio-temporal Approaches: Geographic Objects and Change Process

PLANTIN Jean-Christophe
Participatory Mapping

VENTRE Daniel
Chinese Cybersecurity and Defense

2013

BERNIK Igor
Cybercrime and Cyberwarfare

CAPET Philippe, DELAVALLADE Thomas
Information Evaluation

LEBRATY Jean-Fabrice, LOBRE-LEBRATY Katia
Crowdsourcing: One Step Beyond

SALLABERRY Christian
Geographical Information Retrieval in Textual Corpora

2012

BUCHER Bénédicte, LE BER Florence
Innovative Software Development in GIS

GAUSSIER Eric, YVON François
Textual Information Access

STOCKINGER Peter
Audiovisual Archives: Digital Text and Discourse Analysis

VENTRE Daniel
Cyber Conflict

2011

BANOS Arnaud, THÉVENIN Thomas
Geographical Information and Urban Transport Systems

DAUPHINÉ André
Fractal Geography

LEMBERGER Pirmin, MOREL Mederic
Managing Complexity of Information Systems

STOCKINGER Peter
Introduction to Audiovisual Archives

STOCKINGER Peter
Digital Audiovisual Archives

VENTRE Daniel
Cyberwar and Information Warfare

2010

BONNET Pierre
Enterprise Data Governance

BRUNET Roger
Sustainable Geography

CARREGA Pierre
Geographical Information and Climatology

CAUVIN Colette, ESCOBAR Francisco, SERRADJ Aziz
Thematic Cartography – 3-volume series
Thematic Cartography and Transformations – Volume 1
Cartography and the Impact of the Quantitative Revolution – Volume 2
New Approaches in Thematic Cartography – Volume 3

LANGLOIS Patrice
Simulation of Complex Systems in GIS

MATHIS Philippe
Graphs and Networks – 2nd edition

THERIAULT Marius, DES ROSIERS François
Modeling Urban Dynamics

2009

BONNET Pierre, DETAVERNIER Jean-Michel, VAUQUIER Dominique
Sustainable IT Architecture: the Progressive Way of Overhauling Information Systems with SOA

PAPY Fabrice
Information Science

RIVARD François, ABOU HARB Georges, MERET Philippe
The Transverse Information System

ROCHE Stéphane, CARON Claude
Organizational Facets of GIS

2008

BRUGNOT Gérard
Spatial Management of Risks

FINKE Gerd
Operations Research and Networks

GUERMOND Yves
Modeling Process in Geography

KANEVSKI Michael
Advanced Mapping of Environmental Data

MANOUVRIER Bernard, LAURENT Ménard
Application Integration: EAI, B2B, BPM and SOA

PAPY Fabrice
Digital Libraries

2007

DOBESCH Hartwig, DUMOLARD Pierre, DYRAS Izabela
Spatial Interpolation for Climate Data

SANDERS Lena
Models in Spatial Analysis

2006

CLIQUET Gérard
Geomarketing

CORNIOU Jean-Pierre
Looking Back and Going Forward in IT

DEVILLERS Rodolphe, JEANSOULIN Robert
Fundamentals of Spatial Data Quality

Printed and bound by CPI Group (UK) Ltd, Croydon, CR0 4YY